EFFECTIVE TEAMWORKING
IN THE PROJECT MANAGEMENT
ENVIRONMENT:

EFFECTIVE TEAMWORKING IN THE PROJECT MANAGEMENT ENVIRONMENT:

NURTURING DIVERSITY AND COOPERATION

Edited by

SUE CARTWRIGHT
Manchester School of Management
University of Manchester
Institute of Science & Technology, UK

and

ANDREW GALE
Department of Building Engineering
University of Manchester
Institute of Science & Technology, UK

TUDOR

© S. Cartwright and A. Gale 1996

This version first published in Great Britain by Tudor Business Publishing Limited.
Sole distributors worldwide, Hodder and Stoughton (Publishers) Ltd, 338 Euston Road
London NW1 3BH

A CIP catalogue record for this book is available from the British Library

ISBN 1 872807 81 X

The right of the authors of this work has been asserted by them in accordance with the
Copyright, Designs and Patents Act 1988.

Typeset by Deltatype Ltd, Ellesmere Port, Cheshire
Printed and bound by Athenaeum Press, Ltd.,
Gateshead, Tyne & Wear.

Contents

Acknowledgements

The editors would like to thank Paula Farr and Caroline Wright for their secretarial support and Vera Sokolovski for her graphic skills.

They would like to specially acknowledge the hard work of the Association of Project Managers Specific Interest Group, "Women in Project Management", for designing and running their inaugural one day conference entitled "How Effective is your Organization at Teamworking?" during November 1994 at UMIST in Manchester, UK. This conference would not have been viable without the significant sponsorship received from British Rail Projects and Gleeds Management Services.

Finally, the editors wish to thank all the other authors for their prompt and rigorous submissions which have assisted the early publication of this book.

List of Contributors

Dr Sue Cartwright is a Senior Research Fellow/Honorary Lecturer in Organizational Psychology and Deputy Director of the Centre for Business Psychology at the Manchester School of Management, University of Manchester Institute of Science and Technology. She has published extensively in the area of organizational culture and the cultural dynamics of organizations, as well as the field of occupational stress. She has also worked with a number of organizations on teambuilding initiatives.

Dr Marilyn Davidson is a Senior Lecturer in Organizational Psychology at the Manchester School of Management, University of Manchester Institute of Science and Technology. She has conducted considerable research into the problems faced by women at work and occupational stress.

Dr Andrew Gale is a Lecturer in Construction Management in the Department of Building Engineering and Director of European Construction Ventures Limited (a UMIST Ventures joint venture company) at the University of Manchester Institute of Science and Technology. He has published extensively in the area of women in construction and has worked for the European Commission in Russia devising and delivering management development programmes for the construction sector.

Dr Elin Kvande is Associate Professor of Sociology in the Department of Social and Political Science at the University of Trondheim, Norway. She has undertaken research on female graduate engineers in work organizations, unemployment and paternity leave and is currently engaged in studying gender and organizations and change. She has published many articles on these subjects.

Professor Peter Thompson is the AMEC Professor in the Department of Civil and Structural Engineering at the University of Manchester Institute of Science and Technology. He is an acknowledged expert in project management in the construction sector. He has carried out a number of research projects on project management.

Mr Anthony Reid is Chair of the Association of Project Managers, Specific Interest Group: "Project Organizations and Team Working". He is also principal of the firm: Management Achievement. He has devised, developed and run management training particularly in the field of project management and team building for several years.

Dr Bente Rasmussen is a social scientist from the University of Amsterdam and is currently an Associate Professor at the University of Trondheim. She has studied technological changes at work and union strategies in industry and offices and recently women and computer science within higher education. Since 1985 she has worked on research projects with Elin Kvande and is currently studying decentralization in service organizations together with her.

Foreword

This book brings together hitherto disparate concepts and analyses in order to explore human aspects of project management. So much of what is written on the subject of project management is concerned directly with techniques and systems. When people are mentioned, often rather out-of-date motivation and leadership theories are advanced. This book presents specially commissioned papers given at a one day conference. The editors have introduced these "essays", reported on participant reaction and drawn conclusions in order to set a research agenda. The first paper deals with the role of project management and the nature of project teams and teamworking. The second paper addresses issues associated with the under-representation of women in management and the third synthesises aspects of both by relating organizational teams and gender. Many of the ideas and concepts discussed will seem radical and new to a lot of practising project managers. One of the aims of publishing the papers from this interesting conference is to generate a debate and broaden awareness on the subject of effective teamworking in the context of project management.

1

Editorial Introduction
Effective Teamworking in the Project Environment: Current Issues

Sue Cartwright and Andrew Gale

Introduction

The skills and techniques of project management are increasingly being applied across a wide and diverse range of traditional and new industries. Industries such as construction, engineering, petrochemicals, power, utilities and defence have a long association with project management techniques. However, more recently, project-based teams have become a feature of many service industries such as finance, health, insurance, training, IT and consultancy. As organizations face up to the challenges of a rapidly changing and increasingly complex economic, social, technical and global business environment, the inherent disciplines of project management, and in particular the teamworking aspects, are gaining prominence.

Effective teamworking is important in any organizational context. For any group or team to work effectively and pool its resources, it is recognized that it has to progress through a distinct developmental cycle. Team members have to get to know each other, recognize and accept individual strengths and weaknesses, co-ordinate their activities and establish agreed patterns of working and leadership. It is widely accepted that this involves at least four developmental and temporal stages described by Tuckman (1965) as forming, storming, norming and performing.

However, given the inherent characteristics of the project environment, most notably the time constraints and associated financial costs and penalties, the members of project management teams face considerable and crucial pressure to accelerate this process of group development to mature and perform at an optimal level. Typically, project teams consist of individuals from different functional units and professions, who are assigned responsibility for a temporary and usually pre-determined period of time to successfully complete a particular undertaking. Once this has been achieved the team is disbanded and its members are reassigned.

The dynamic, non-static nature of project mangement is reflected in the following characteristics commonly associated with the project environment:

- non-routine "one-off" jobs for which there is no precedent and hence no established systems and procedures
- the input and co-ordination of different people and resources which need to be asembled quickly
- a very short (and often expensive) learning curve
- operating under considerable time pressures and at the same time high quality demands
- high visibility of the project and the project management team
- a high potential for conflict and ambiguity.

The Demands for Teamworking

Research has consistently demonstrated (Thamhain and Wilemon 1974; Andrews and Tjosvold 1983; Kerzner 1982) that conflict is a common and frequent feature of the project environment. Based on a study of 135 project team engineers, Barker, Tjosvold and Andrews (1988) concluded:

> the variety of professions represented, the use of group problem solving, the pressure to reach consensus, the ambiguity of authority and the varied demands placed on all members, all mean that the project manager and members will continually face conflict.

Consequently, the role of the project manager is often that of conflict manager. Whilst the criteria for a "successful" project are accepted as being universally similar: *time, cost, quality* (Cartwright and Gale 1995), the priority placed on these may vary between team members and/or different stages in the project life cycle. The evidence of a study of 150 project managers (Thamhain and Wilemon 1975) suggests that most conflicts occur over work schedules, responsibilities and time management issues rather than cost.

Furthermore, whilst the project environment of itself may have a high propensity for conflict, it has also to be considered within the wider context of the organizational or occupational culture in which it functions, which may also be conflictual. There is a growing body of research (Gale and Cartwright 1995; Gale 1992, 1990; Greed 1991) which suggests that the culture of the construction industry, a traditional project-based industry, is characterized by crisis, conflict and masculinity. The construction industry is demonstrably male; not only the gender of its workforce, but the prevailing culture, ethos and values of the industry are "masculine" in orientation. Consequently, it promotes and rewards individualistic rather than collective effort and behaviours.

Almost ten years ago (Hastings, Bixby and Chaudhry-Lawton 1986) a report on a world congress on project management found that over 70 per cent of delegates considered that the most crucial area of current interest to project management was "educating the Project Management team in the human aspects of Project Management". Since then, the technology, software and technical systems associated with project management have become increasingly more sophisticated, yet the challenges of making the team, that is "the human systems", work effectively still remain.

Background to the Book
The continuing change in emphasis from individual to team means that project managers need to increase their awareness of the human aspects of project management and team effectiveness. In recognition, the Women in Project Management Special Interest Group, as part of the Association of Project Managers, held an inaugural one-day conference entitled "How effective is your organization at teamworking?" at the University of Manchester Institute of Science and Technology, on 11 November 1994. The conference was chaired by Tim Carter, Partner of Davis, Langdon and Everest and Vice President of the Association of Project Managers. The conference was sponsored by British Rail Projects and Gleeds Management Services.

This volume brings together the three papers which were specifically commissioned for this conference. The papers presented had common themes and discussed contradictions in theoretical and empirical evidence on organizations, projects and their environments, gender and the gendering of project and organizational cultures, and aspects of management and leadership. Delegates were encouraged to discuss these contributions and the issues they raised in depth in the workshop sessions incorporated in the proceedings. The main points arising from these workshops, which reflect the response of the delegates in the specific context of their day-to-day experiences in the project environment have been also included in this book.

Although gender was a strong theme of the conference, this book does not seek to align itself exclusively with the women in management literature but rather to address the issue of accommodating, managing and nurturing diversity in project teams for the optimal benefit of team performance and team members.

In this respect, this book is substantially different from most other published conference proceedings in approaching the subject from a multi-disciplinary perspective, which combines both academic and practitioner viewpoints. The project environment provides a challenging opportunity for further research into teamworking. As different projects develop different cultures and different ways of doing things, studies of the project environment can also usefully extend our understanding of the influence of gender and gender-related values on the development of culture and its influence on the behaviour of team members.

Contents of the Book
The opening paper of the conference was given by Peter Thompson, AMEC Professor of Engineering Project Management, UMIST. This paper forms the basis of Chapter 2, which discusses the historical background, development and role of project management today. The key issues arising from this chapter are concerned with accountability, the selection and establishment of project teams, incentives and communication. The selection of individual team members is the logical first step in putting together an effective team. Drawing heavily on his experiences in the oil, gas, chemical and process industries, Thompson argues for the need to form two distinct project teams linked to the definable phases of projects – appraisal, implementation and completion. He also emphasises that quality in the context of management of complex and high risk projects is essentially the quality of the people involved, not the systems employed.

The majority of project management teams, certainly within traditional project-based industries, tend to attract an exclusively male membership. Despite recent initiatives to increase the number of women entering the engineering and construction industry, women continue to be significantly under-represented in industries and business sectors which have been traditionally regarded as stereotypically "male" occupations, the very industries which employ project management techniques and demand a diversity of creative talents and expertise. According to the Department of Employment, women's representation in the UK construction industry is less than one per cent and in science and engineering less than nine per cent (Gale and Cartwright 1995).

The following chapter (Chapter 3) by Dr Marilyn Davidson challenges the reasons why women continue to be under-represented in management generally and in project teams specifically. In discussing the barriers facing women at work and entering the labour market, she makes the point that in the past there has been far too much emphasis on women trying to "fit in" to organizations and adopt the attitudes and behaviours of male colleagues and team members. Increasing the number of women in the workplace may have a positive effect for the enhancement of women at work but it needs to be reinforced by a change in attitudes and a more gender-inclusive working environment and culture. It would appear that project-based industries, like construction, are "fishing in only half an ocean" by not recruiting women. Further, by attracting a higher proportion of women into the male domain of project management, men may also benefit from the changes in culture necessary and caused. More "different" men may also be attracted to project management. In this sense, what is good for women is good for men (Gale 1991).

The performance of project teams and their individual members cannot be separated from the influence of the wider environment in which the team have to operate. Therefore, the next chapter (Chapter 4) by Professor Elin Kvande and Bente Rasmussen, introduces a more macro-level of analysis in discussing the influence of organizational structures, politics and cultures on the gendering of organizations and its implications for the project environment. Based on a study of male and female engineers in six industries in Norway, Kvande and Rasmussen differentiate between two types of organization – static hierarchies and dynamic networks. Static hierarchies are described as an old fashioned system in which older males maintain patriarchal power relations. In contrast, dynamic network organizations are ones in which emphasis is placed on the professionalism and expertise which organizational or team members can potentially contribute to the task irrespective of their sex. Whilst dynamic networks are potentially more conducive to effective teamworking, unfortunately it would seem that they are not generally characteristic of the project environment today, at least within the UK.

Chapter 5 reports on the workshop session following the papers constituting Chapters 2 and 3. Delegates worked in teams, allocated by the conference organizers. Each team had a different theme. These were intended to enable delegates to discuss issues arising from the first part of the conference. Teams were encouraged to represent the views of all members, not a consensus or majority view.

The conference organizers had spent several hours role-playing the workshop idea themselves. As a result, on the conference day they knew exactly what they, as a team, wanted from the workshops. Workshop teams presented their "findings". These were innovative and fun. Some elected a spokesperson, others performed as a whole with posters and graphics. An important feature of the workshop session was that it gathered practitioner responses to the research-based academic papers presented.

Finally, Chapter 6 attempts to draw together the major themes and issues raised by the contributors and structure them into a meaningful research agenda for the future.

References

Andrews, I R and Tjosvold, D (1983). "Conflict management under different levels of conflict intensity", *Journal of Occupational Behaviour, Vol. 4,* 223–228.

Barker, J, Tjosvold, D and Andrews, I R (1988). "Conflict approaches of effective and ineffective Project Managers: A field study in the matrix organization", *Journal of Management Studies, Vol. 25 (2),* March.

Cartwright, S and Gale, A W (1995). "Project Management: Different Gender, Different Culture", *The Leadership and*

Organizational Development Journal, 16. (4).

Gale, A W (1990). "Women in Construction – Comparative survey of women and men in construction, engineering and the banking and finance industries" in *Proceedings of the 1990 GASAT Conference*, Jonkoping, Sweden, May, 63–72.

Gale, A W (1992). "The construction industry's male culture must feminize if conflict is to be reduced: The role of education as gatekeeper to a male construction industry", in *Construction Conflict: Management and Resolution*, Fenn, P and Gameson R (eds) E and F N Spon, 416–427.

Gale, A W and Cartwright, S (1995). "Women in Project Management: Entry into a male domain", *The Leadership and Organizational Development Journal, 16, (2)*.

Greed, C (1991). *Surveying sisters, women in a traditional male profession*. London, Routledge, 51.

Hastings, C, Bixby, P and Chaudhry-Lawton, R (1986). *Superteams – A Blue Print for Organizational Success*. Fontana/ Collins.

Kerzner, H (1982). *Project Management for Executives*. Van Nostrand Reinhold Co.

Thamhain, H J and Wilemon, D L (1974). "Conflict management in project oriented work environments", in *Proceedings of the Project Management Institute*, Drexel Hill, Pensylvania.

Tuckman, B W (1965). "Developmental sequence in small groups", *Psychological Bulletin*.

2

The Role of Project Management in our Changing Society

Peter Thompson

Introduction

The author briefly considers the historical background to the development and procurement of projects in the engineering construction industry with emphasis on practice in the civil, process and offshore sectors. He then considers the transition from a fragmented ill-disciplined industry serving mainly public clients to the well-ordered, broad-based and forward-looking team serving private sector clients in a rapidly changing and uncertain commercial environment.

The issue of teamwork is addressed from the client's point of view, together with the evolution of the project manager as his representative. The way in which different contractual systems, ranging from the traditional approach through to partnering, meet the client's requirements are explored. The quality of the individual team member is discussed and the essential attributes of the project manager defined.

Background

The traditional procedure for procurement of projects in the building and civil engineering industries originated from the needs of public works. Here the client defined requirements based on longterm predictions of demand in a relatively static society and with little attention to commercial issues. The client would delegate design to an architect or engineer, award a construction contract to a contractor and entrust the co-ordination and administration of design and construction to the architect and/or engineer. The whole process incorporated the concept of minimum price and separated the client from contractors.

This philosophy coupled with the fragmentation of the design and construction process generated conflict and ultimately led to the development of the claims industry. The increased use of subcontracts and the introduction of additional specialized professionals into the project environment generated a multitude of interfaces with which the simple traditional procedures could not cope. The architect or engineer was appointed on the basis of technical competence, not management capability. In consequence, there has been a general lack of definition of requirement by the client and a lack of discipline by professionals. The emphasis was upon resolution of conflict not the avoidance of conflict by collaborative planning.

The Banwell and Harris initiatives generated modest improvement in industry performance. Both reports related to construction management in the public sector with little emphasis on the overall client role or the private sector. In the late 1980s and early 1990s Europe experienced a period of rapid political, environmental and technical change. The industry saw the introduction of management contracting, design and build and an emphasis on fast-tracking. It was, however, still slow to recognize the true client requirement.

Meanwhile, in the competitive commercial world of the process industry with a short-term market for a product and the relative importance of early penetration of the market, there was greater input by the client on conceptual design, early procurement and detailed planning. It was here that we saw the evolution of the project manager as the person responsible and accountable for managing the investment on behalf of the client. Project teams were later responsible for the realization of innovative and complex defence initiatives. In the offshore petroleum industry where massive projects are exposed to even greater technical and market risks (Gaisford 1986), the concept of a single partnership team integrating the expertise of client and contractor is now proving attractive.

We are now experiencing the implications of free market forces, greater competition and global players (Lazlo 1990) with greater uncertainty generating a need for rapid response to opportunities based on timely commercial decisions. This demands flexibility in project concept and detailed design, greater attention to the environment and to health and safety, all of which demand well-informed client involvement. In many cases priority is given to quality and to timely completion rather than cheapest price. Construction is gradually experiencing a transition from a fragmented, ill-disciplined industry which frequently infuriated clients to a well-ordered, efficient, and forward-looking team activity.

The Client's Role and Requirements

A) THE PROJECT

A project is a temporary activity. In the context of this paper it is a phase in the development and procurement of some new facility, a structure, a manufacturing plant, a software system or maybe an offshore production unit. A client invests in a project to generate benefit to the organization or to the community that it serves. It is a temporary activity spanning appraisal and implementation of the facility. The client initiates the project, and later assumes responsibility, as the owner, for the operation and maintenance of the enterprise. The associated project cashflow is typically as Fig. 1.

Investment in an engineering project also involves risk. In the author's opinion the success or failure of the enterprise will depend crucially on the identification, understanding and

PROJECT ACCOUNT BALANCE

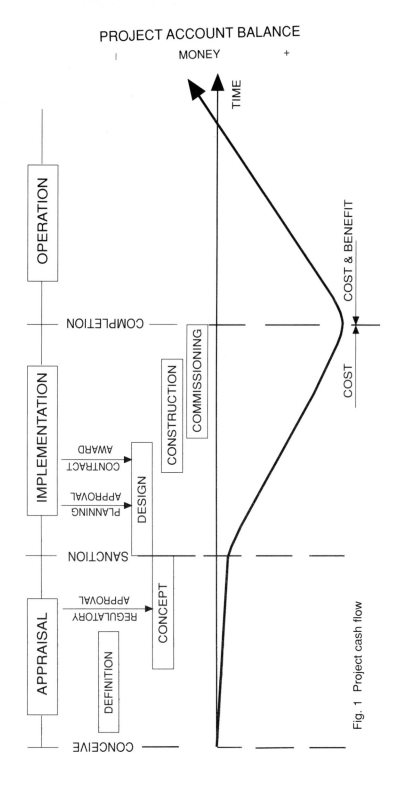

Fig. 1 Project cash flow

management of uncertainty (Thompson and Perry 1992). In most engineering projects relatively modest expenditure is incurred during the appraisal stage, followed by rapid expenditure during project implementation. The characteristics of the implementation phase of engineering projects are, typically:

- specific objectives
- temporary organization and team
- rapid expenditure
- demanding time-scale
- numerous collaborating organizations
- uncertainty/financial risk
- impact on the public and/or the environment.

It is most important to note that the client does not derive any benefit from the investment until the project is operational and that the organization's maximum exposure to risk occurs at the time of peak investment. The client's role throughout the project development and implementation is crucial to its success, but it is widely held that the project manager frequently lacks top-level support (Fahlen 1990).

b) THE PROJECT SCENARIO
The individual project, however significant and potentially beneficial to the client organization, will only constitute part of corporate business. Appraisal and implementation of the project are only temporary activities.

The relationship between the ongoing parent, or corporate, organization and the temporary project is illustrated in Fig. 2 (Thompson 1990). The nature and functioning of this relationship is of prime importance to the project team.

c) THE CLIENT'S REQUIREMENTS
Although the specific technical requirements will vary from project to project, the author suggests that the overall client requirements include:

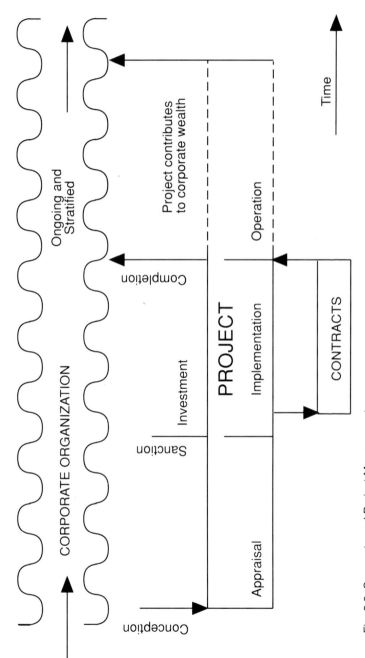

Fig. 2.2 Corporate and Project Management
New projects are essential to the continuing
prosperity of the corporate organization

- minimum investment, maximum benefit
- confidence in estimates/predictions
- an acceptable level of risk
- fitness for purpose
- value for money
- partnership not conflict.

A survey conducted during recent research (Godfrey 1994) concluded that "teamwork" encapsulates much of what clients require from their professional advisors: respect, commitment, confidence, support, etc.

> A period of getting to know each other . . . Building up a working relationship and a level of trust . . . It is quite important to understand what the incentives of both us and the contractors are, and try and get the two to come together somehow. A relationship such that they recognize that we are there to help the contractor to achieve our objectives.
>
> I want them to work closely together . . . I want a close-knit team, a team response. Jobs that have gone wrong, in my experience, have been where there has been no teamwork. Trust, empathy, sympathy . . . all those things, but teamwork.

d) THE CLIENT'S ROLE

The general requirement is for the client to give clear direction to those responsible for development and implementation of the project. Initially this will involve agreement of clear objectives, priorities and scope which must subsequently be reviewed regularly to take account of possible changes in the project or market environment.

Most importantly, the client must give timely decisions. The author suggests that it is the client, as investor, who must also drive the project to a successful conclusion. This may prove difficult where the corporate organization has a rigid hierarchical management structure linked to slowly changing long-term objectives. Managers of engineering projects will frequently encounter a mixture of technical, environmental, logistical and physical problems together with levels of risk and uncertainty which are rarely encountered in day-to-day line management. The style of management required for such work will therefore differ in many ways from that required in the relatively static surroundings of traditional line management. In all but the smallest enterprise the client will be best served by the establishment of a team dedicated to the setting and achievement of realistic project objectives. In the author's opinion, the project director and/or project manager should be in-house appointments (Ninos 1986).

The Client Team
The likely interaction of the established client corporate organization, typically structured in departments, and the temporary project activity is illustrated in Fig. 3. Study of this diagram suggests that it is unlikely that a single team will prove appropriate or effective for both the appraisal and implementation phases of the project.

A) DURING APPRAISAL
Project appraisal is a process of investigation, review and evaluation undertaken as the project, or alternative concepts of the project, are defined. This study is designed to help the client to make informed and rational choices about the nature and scale of investment in the project. The core of the process is an economic evaluation of all costs and benefits that can be valued in monetary terms, that is also, therefore, called a cost/benefit analysis. Appraisal is likely to be a cyclic process repeated as new ideas are developed, additional information is received, and uncertainty is reduced, until the client is able to make the critical decision to sanction implementation of the project and commit the investment in expectation of the predicted return.

The greatest degree of uncertainty about the future and the outcome of the project is encountered at this stage, and the appraisal is essentially a process of risk reduction (Thompson and Perry 1992). It is also largely an internal matter for the client organization involving confidential commercial decisions but consultation and support of external bodies will frequently be necessary.

Consequently it is likely that several internal departments, typically those shown in Fig. 3, will contribute to

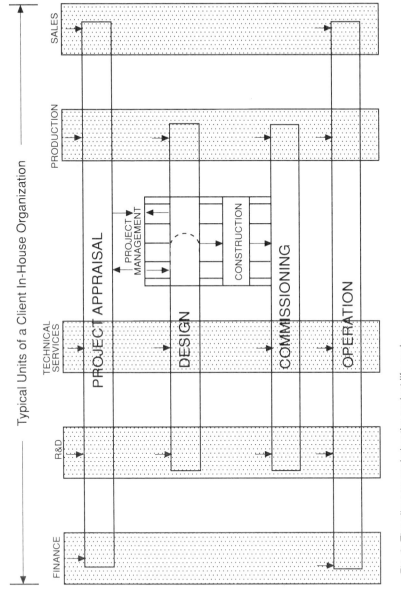

Fig. 3 The client team during the project life-cycle

requirements, estimates and predictions. The author suggests that the leaders of this representative group should constitute the project board (Ninos 1986), who should oversee appraisal and implementation and also commissioning and handover for operation. In this way they will remain accountable to the client.

The project manager should contribute to the appraisal and be a member of this team and be well informed of the politics and debate surrounding the key decisions made at this time. There are however many situations where the project manager for the implementation phase is not the appropriate person to lead the appraisal team. This may best be done by the project director (Ninos 1986). A key function of this leader will be to integrate and moderate the aspirations of the various contributing departments and to ensure that the proposal submitted for sanction best meets the client's stated objectives.

In the rapidly changing economic, social and technical environment of the 1990s, regular reappraisal of all aspects of project development is strongly advocated by the author as part of the audit and review process. The implications for project management of changes in the market are likely to be particularly significant. This review should ideally involve the members of the broad-based project board responsible for the original appraisal, not the project implementation team.

The author concludes therefore that a strong project board, which represents all the interests of the client, should be established to take responsibility for appraisal and to oversee implementation and eventual commissioning and handover of the asset for operation.

b) DURING IMPLEMENTATION

The organization established for detailed design, procurement, construction and erection and commissioning of the project will require a diverse range of skills, largely different from those utilized during appraisal. In most cases many external organizations will be involved under contract to the client.

The role of the project manager and the team is now to achieve the objectives defined by the client at sanction, and to protect the client's interests. Responsibilities will normally include:

- determination of the contract strategy
- award of contracts
- overall planning of implementation and regular review of performance
- management of the interface between client and all other parties
- assessment and control of the issue of change orders and variations
- planning and management of commissioning and handover of the completed project
- public relations.

The client's team may or may not be involved in the day-to-day administration of the contracts, depending on the strategy selected (Perry 1985). In the traditional approach they are likely to take responsibility for integration of a series of individual contracts for different types of work, for example civil/ building works, plant supply and installation, IT systems – although management of design and construction for each package may be delegated to the relevant architect or engineer. When target or cost reimbursable contracts are employed, normally for high risk or ill-defined projects (Perry and Thompson 1980), the client team will be directly involved in day-to-day decision making. Where a management contracting, design and build, or a turnkey approach is adopted, another organization is introduced to manage design and construction. In a partnering alliance contract a single integrated team will be formed.

Referring again to Fig. 2, the project management team established for implementation will be different in nature, organization and attitude to the parent organization and to the project board. If it is to achieve demanding objectives in the demanding conditions listed above it must be dynamic, forward-looking, meticulous and decisive. Both teams must display the same positive attitude.

It is essential that all communication between the client (and separate departments) and the contractors is channelled through the project management team. Direct contact between departments, each with their own requirement of the project, and the contractor, is known to result in confusion, disruption, delay and extra cost. The project manager cannot however manage the project in isolation from the commercial world in which the company is operating: decisions must be related to current market forecasts and the changing external environment. The project manager must also be party to the review carried out by the broad-based project board advocated above. As the project nears completion the project manager must initiate the commissioning procedures and organize handover of the completed project to the operating disciplines.

Teamwork and the Procurement of Design and Construction
If one accepts that the benefits of teamwork include:

● use of established and proven systems and procedures
● confidence in the performance of team members
● ease of communication

then the traditional approach to the procurement of design and construction is likely to fail in all these key areas.

In most cases, although some effort is devoted to selecting a capable contractor, the dominant criterion is lowest bid price. Consequently the client is likely to engage a different group of designers, suppliers and contractors for each successive project. New working relationships have to be established for each project. Success is a matter of hard work and chance and in many cases conflict ensues. It is not surprising that the recent Latham Report advocates new approaches to the construction of the project team and supports NEC and the greater use of partnering (Latham 1944).

Teamwork and Project Management
The author believes that the early appointment of a project director and/or project manager to pursue the client's interest

in a potential project is advisable and that, in most cases, they will need the support of a select team. Teamwork is at the core of effective project management. The establishment of a project team however will not in itself ensure success or harmony.

Teamwork involves the effective co-operation of a group of people in their activities directed towards a common goal. The essence of teamwork is that the performance of the group as a whole is greater than would be the normal sum of the performance of the individuals comprising the group. It follows that project management involves team building since it is fundamentally a team activity. It is not concerned with the continuing operation of an organization, but with effective action by a disparate group of people with different objectives harnessed to a common goal. The team itself, however, cannot be maintained indefinitely and is itself subject to the same changes as a project. There is a limited time for which the synergy of the team can be maintained. The important thing is to limit the time-span of projects to within the maximum life-span of a team by phasing the project, and dividing the responsibility. In the view of Gabriel, three years is the maximum period for which a project can be satisfactorily controlled and the team approach maintained. Therefore it follows that to be controllable, major projects should be split into three-year phases or sub-divisions (Gabriel 1991).

Quality

In the context of project management, quality of performance of the project is greatly dependent on the quality of project staff. Projects and contracts are managed by people who are continuously directing and communicating with other human beings. Great attention must be paid to the selection and motivation of staff. Personality and ability to think ahead are as important as technical know-how. Risk and uncertainty which results in change is perhaps the single crucial difference between line management and project management. Individual members of the team must not therefore be risk-averse. The author considers that the following personal attributes are desirable.

ATTITUDE	– positive, forward looking
JUDGEMENT	– capable of decision making in uncertain conditions
ABILITY TO ADAPT TO CHANGE	– understand human behaviour and
COLLABORATE AS MEMBERS OF TEAM	communicate effectively.

Project and contract management staff must be given adequate authority to manage in their dynamic working environment without continual reference to higher management.

Care must be taken to ensure that the adoption of a quality assurance system does not result in rigid adherence to unnecessarily demanding specifications. Neither must the system inhibit the flexibility and judgement required for the management of the uncertainties associated with the one-off job.

The concept of total quality management and the desired continuous improvement of personal performance will only be achieved if team members are stimulated by appropriate and timely training and allowed to utilize their ingenuity and imagination. The author believes that, having selected staff of the appropriate calibre, "project-related" training given at the time of formation of the project team will motivate and make a considerable contribution to subsequent effective teamwork. Frequently, in his experience, this training is either inadequate or is given too late.

Partnering and Alliance Contracts
Partnering and alliance contracts are being developed to promote and enhance teamwork between clients and their contractors. To date they have been used mainly in the United States and in the UK process and offshore industries. They are all one-off arrangements which provide a single integrated team for management and engineering of the project.

As teamwork is the essence of these contracts particular

attention must be given to the selection, composition and functioning of the team, and appointment of contractors on the sole criterion of minimum price is not appropriate. It is normal for the contracts to incorporate a common incentive for all parties related to the final cost, duration and/or performance of the completed project. This emphasis on the final outcome of the contract is likely to prove far more effective than competition on initial bid price, which inevitably increases. The author has experience of several contracts of this type and strongly supports the view of Sir Michael Latham (Latham 1944), that extension of their use to other areas of construction activity should be investigated.

Conclusions
Management is concerned with the setting and achievement of realistic objectives for the project or contract. This increasingly demands greater effort – it will not happen as a matter of course –and it will require the dedication and motivation of people. The provision and training of an adequate project management team is therefore an essential for a successful job. It is their drive and judgement, their ability to persuade and lead, which will ensure that the project objectives are achieved.

References
Fahlen, L (1990). "The role of the managing director in a customer orientating project", *in Proceedings of Internet 90, Vol. 2* Vienna, Austria.
Gabriel, E (1991). "Teamwork – Fact and Fiction", *International Journal Project Management, Vol. 9, No. 4*, 195–198.
Gaisford, R W (1990). "Project Management in North Sea Construction". *International Journal of Project Management*, Vol. 4, No. 1, 5–12.
Godfrey, P (1994). "The Control of Risk". *In Proceedings of Risk, Management & Procurement in Construction*. London.
Laszlo, E (1990). "Responsible (project) management in an

unstable world" in *Handbook of Management by Projects*. Manz, Austria, 16–21.

Latham, Sir M (1944). *Constructing the Team* HMSO.

Ninos, F E and Wearne, S H (1986). "Control of projects during construction". *In Proceedings of ICE, Part 1, 80*. August.

Perry J G (1985). "The Development of Contract Strategies for Construction Projects". *PhD Thesis, UMIST*.

Perry J G and Thompson, P A (1980). "A Guide to Target and Cost-Reimbursable Construction Contracts". *Report 85, CIRIA*, London.

Project Managers and their teams: Selection, Education, Careers (1990) in Proceedings of the Proc. 14th INTERNET INTERNATIONAL. Expert Seminar, Zurich.

Semolic, B (1990). "Strategic management and projects", *in Proceedings of Internet 90, Vol. 2*. Austria.

Thompson, P A (1990). "The Client role in Project Management". *In Proceedings of Internet 90, Vol 2*, Vienna, Austria.

Thompson, P A and Perry J G (eds) (1992). Engineering Construction Risks – *A Guide to Project Risk Analysis and Risk Management*. Thomas Telford Ltd.

Wearne S H (ed) (1989). *Control of Engineering Projects*, 2nd ed. Thomas Telford Ltd.

3

Women in Management: Why the Glass Ceiling's Not Cracking

Marilyn Davidson

Today, in most Western countries, organizations recognize that women represent a significant proportion of the labour force. In Britain, women now comprise 44 per cent of people in paid employment and between 1979 and 1989 the number of women in employment increased by 1.6 million or 17 per cent. Moreover, the percentage of women with dependent children who were economically active rose from 47 per cent to 59 per cent (Commission of the European Communities 1993). Similar trends are evident in Australasia, the USA, Canada, and throughout Europe (Davidson and Cooper 1992, 1993). In the European labour market, women now make up 41 per cent of all adults who are in work or looking for work (Commission of the European Communities 1993). Nevertheless, occupational segregation by gender still persists in all European labour markets. More than 50 per cent of employed women are found in service or clerical jobs, compared with 20 per cent of men. According to Rubery and Fagan (1993), the majority of the new jobs women moved into in the 1980s were in two occupational areas: professional jobs and clerical jobs. Therefore, while an increasing number of women are entering the lower level service and clerical jobs which are already female dominated, some women are gaining access to highly skilled professional jobs, including management, (Rubery and Fagan 1993).

Recent evidence in Britain suggests that, at school, girls are attaining better academic examination results than boys. The 1994 National Consortium for Examination Results showed that, for the first time, girls achieved better 'A' Level results than boys, and more girls than boys achieved grade A. Girls were also ten points ahead of boys for the second year running at GCSE Level and girls and boys were level in subjects such as maths and science with girls excelling in language-based subjects – this despite the set back of continuous assessment of course work which was suggested by some to favour girls over boys. (Apparently, this phenomenon is not new and girls have always done better than boys, so the threshold for passing the former 11 plus examination was set higher for girls than boys!)

Not surprisingly there have also been significant increases in the number of females going into higher education. In 1983, for example, women in Britain constituted 41 per cent of university undergraduates and 32 per cent of postgraduates, compared with 44 per cent and 37 per cent respectively in 1989. There are also increasing trends for women graduates to move into areas of managerial and professional employment which were previously dominated by men. In 1973, only ten per cent of students studying for social administration and business degrees were women, whereas today in the UK more than 45 per cent of these students are female (Davidson and Cooper 1992). A recent survey of ten UK companies who kept detailed records of their graduate intake over the last ten years found that Shell had tripled the number of women graduates it recruits, while Unilever had more than doubled its intake. Other companies such as National Westminster Bank, Barclays, ICL, Coopers and Lybrand, and Abbey National,

Table 1:   Women as a proportion of overall UK graduate intake

SHELL		BRITISH STEEL		UNILEVER		COOPERS & LYBRAND		NATWEST	
1983	8%	1983	10%	1984	18%	1984	31%	1984	35%
1994	24%	1993	23%	1994	46%	1994	42%	1994	48%
ICL		Abbey National		Barclays		Inst/Chtd Accts		P & Gamble	
1987	39%	1987	43%	1986	36%	1985	26%	1987	27%
1993	65%	1993	54%	1993	59%	1992	37%	1994	37%

Source: Panorama Survey of top ten graduate recruiters from 1983/4 using latest available figures. Webber G (1994) BBC News and Current Affairs Publicity Press Release.

had also seen big increases in the number of graduate women they recruit (Webber 1994; see Table 1).

Fig. 1 illustrates that, in all the EEC countries, women are increasing their share of professional jobs (ie., scientists, nurses, teachers, lawyers, artists, etc). In 1990 women held 64 per cent of these jobs in Denmark compared to 38 per cent in Luxembourg. Even so, the majority of women in professional jobs are still concentrated in the caring professions and the public sector and are occupying the lower managerial positions (Commission of the European Committees 1993).

Fig. 1:   Change in the female share of selected occupational groups, 1983-90

(a) Professional, technical and related occupations

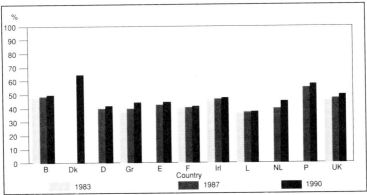

(b) Clerical and related occupations

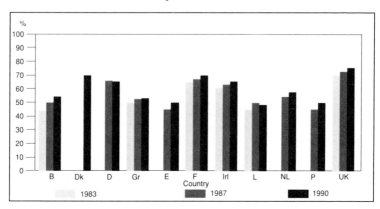

International Standard Classification of Occupations (ISCO 68)

Occupational data from the European Community Labour Force Survey classified into the ISCO 68 major occupational groups can be used to provide a comparative picture of what happened to women's occupational position in the EC over the 1980s.

Major Ocupational Groups	Female/male share of jobs (%)	Concentration of employment women (%)	men (%)
1. Professional, technical & related workers *Scientists, nurses, teachers, lawyers, artists, etc.*	45/55	19	16
2. Administrative and managerial workers *Government administrators plus managers not classified elsewhere.*	23/77	2	4
3. Clerical & related workers *Clerical supervisors, typists, cashiers, telephonists etc.*	64/36	30	11
4. Sales workers *All sales workers, including managers and working proprietors.*	49/51	12	9
5. Service workers *All catering and related workers including managers; personal service workers such as cleaners and hairdressers; the police.*	66/34	20	7
6. Agricultural & related workers *All agricultural and related workers including managers and supervisors.*	34/66	5	7
7. Production, transport, labourers & related workers *Manufacturing and construction workers and supervisors.*	16/84	12	45
Military	*/100	*	1
ALL EMPOYMENTS (EC11)[1]	41/59	100	100

While the evidence suggests that it is relatively easy for women to gain employment at the lower levels of organizations, it is still proving very difficult for them to reach upper middle and senior management positions and the percentage of senior female executives is very small. In Britain, there are approximately three million managers with about a fifth being women; of the million or so middle and senior managers, at most four per cent are women (Davidson and Cooper 1992; Davidson and Burke 1994). The aim of this chapter is to argue that, despite the increasing numbers of women entering the field of management (particularly at the graduate level), the indications are that rather than cracking, the glass ceiling (the invisible but very real barrier that women experience when they vie for promotion) is actually thickening! This is happening regardless of the fact that most of the negative myths associated with women as managers have been shattered. While acknowledging that there is an urgent need for the implementation of effective equal opportunity policies and programmes, what is also required is an emphasis on changing traditional managerial sex and ethic stereotyping.

Women in Business and Management
Table 2 shows the percentage of women in management and business in the European Community and clearly illustrates the concentration of women at the bottom of the managerial hierarchy, with fewer than five per cent in senior management roles (Davidson and Cooper 1993). Furthermore, there is an increasing trend for women to start their own businesses with between 15 per cent and 30 per cent of entrepreneurs or business owners being female. While many of these businesses are small, they are undoubtedly growing in size and number. Indeed, it has been suggested that the control and flexibility that owning your own business provides is a greater attraction to working women, particularly those with children, than any hierarchy-driven, male-dominated, corporate culture.

Women are most likely to be managers in those occupations which are still traditionally female, such as catering and retail. A British Institute of Management (BIM) survey, which

Table 2: Women in management and business in the European Community

Country*	Working Females as a Percentage of all:			
	Managers	Middle Managers	Senior Managers	Entrepreneurs/ Self-employed
UK	26	–	2	25
Eire	17.4	–	–	31.5
Denmark	11	10	5	–
Netherlands	13	18	–	24
Germany	6	–	–	17
France	25	44	4.6	16†
Belgium	–	12.5	5	–
Greece	14	–	8	14
Italy	–	–	3	25
Portugal	–	–	–	–
Spain	10	5	5	37

* Category definitions vary between countries
† Head of firms with 10+ persons
Source: Davidson, M. J. and Cooper, C. L., (eds) (1993)

covered the careers of 1,882 male and female managers, gave further support to those distributions (Nicholson and West 1988). While the majority of both male and female managers were concentrated in the private and service sectors, women were found less in manufacturing than men and were employed more in service organizations (professional services, education, training and government). Women were also more likely to be found in certain managerial occupations, such as personnel, office administration and training, and in organizations where there was a higher than average number of other women.

In the United States, with the strongest legislation affecting the employment of women, this type of gender segregation in management appears to be breaking down at a more rapid rate. The ranks of female managers had tripled during the 1970s and, by 1979, 30.5 per cent of American managers were women. Today, this figure has risen to over 44 per cent (Davidson and Burke 1994). However, despite legislation, American female managers are still finding the glass ceiling difficult to shatter at senior executive level where women constitute around five per cent of managerial positions (a percentage which has hardly changed in the last decade).

Myths Shattered, but is the Glass Ceiling Thickening?
Over the past decade, numerous cross-cultural studies have shattered most of the negative myths commonly instilled in the minds of employers regarding the "unsuitability" of women as managers.

Pregnancy/ Wastage –	Pregnancy is *not* the main reason that women managers leave organizations; they do so because of dissatisfaction with career opportunities (Davidson and Cooper 1992; Homans 1987; Brett and Stroh 1994).
Lack of Ambition –	There are few sex differences regarding achievement, motivation, aspiration towards promotion, or motivation to manage (Davidson and Burke 1994) and some studies have found women managers to be more ambitious than their male counterparts (Nicholson and West 1988).
Poor Commitment –	Some studies have found women managers to be more committed to their careers, as opposed to family or home lives (Lahtinen and Wilson 1994; Powell, Posner and Schmidt 1985).
Lack of Mobility –	Women managers tend to be mobile and more radical in their job changes compared to men. Nicholson and West (1988) found women with children made the more rapid job changes (as well as being highly motivated regarding success, and scored high on dominance, adjustment and need for growth).

Inferior Leadership –	There are far more similarities than differences in the way men and women "manage" and over the last 20 years research has shown that women are as effective as men as managerial leaders (Ferrario 1994; Bourantas and Paplexandris 1990).
Inappropriate Language and Communication Skills –	In the past, there has been an implication that female communication styles have been less effective that men's (for example the emphasis on assertion courses directed at women). However communication skills such as attentiveness, collaboration and supportiveness have been shown to enhance productivity and morale in the work environment. Research findings have consistently shown that women leaders use collaboration and participative communication. Men in general engage in more directive, unilateral communication to exercise leadership, which is consistent with their learned view of talk as a way to assert self and achieve status (Helgesen 1990; Case 1994).

Even so, the realities are that numerous cross-cultural studies have concluded that while managerial women are good at coping with stress, they experience additional unique sources of stress related to their minority status and gender and that these pressures result in higher levels of overall occupational stress compared to their male counterparts (Davidson and Cooper 1982, 1983, 1987, 1992; Davidson, Cooper and Baldini, in Press; Devanna 1987; Greenglass 1985). Overall, research findings indicate that women managers experience more external discriminating based pressures including strains of coping with discrimination, prejudice and sex stereotyping; lack of role models and feelings of isolation; burdens of coping with the role of "token woman", and higher work/home conflict pressures (Davidson and Cooper 1992; Davidson, Cooper and Baldini, in press).

Nevertheless, until recently there had been degrees of optimism in relation to the increasig numbers of women entering various management levels in British organizations over the past two decades. However, this optimism was dramatically dampened by the recent 1994 UK National Management Survey carried out by The Institute of Management and Remuneration Economics, which included a sample of 20,890 employees in 330 organizations.

Table 3 shows that the number of female managers and directors in the UK's largest organizations is on the decline – 9.5 per cent in 1994 compared to 10.2 per cent in 1993. The percentage of women managers has fallen at almost every level of management.

Table 3: Females - Sample size by responsibility level

	1974	1983	1991	1993	1994
Directors	0.6%	0.3%	2.6%	2.8%	2.8%
Functions Heads	0.4%	1.5%	6.1%	6.8%	6.1%
Department Heads	2.1%	1.9%	8.1%	9.0%	8.7%
Section Leader	2.4%	5.3%	11.6%	13.2%	12%
Whole Sample	1.8%	3.3%	8.6%	10.2%	9.5%

Source: Institute of Management and Remuneration Economics (1994)

This survey also confirmed that the average profile of the female manager compared to her male counterpart has hardly changed over the past decade. She earns less – the average female manager earns £27,862 compared to £32,303 earned by the average male manager. Even at director level, the average female earns £56,040 compared to her male colleagues who earn £74,987. Only 51.6 per cent of female managers have company cars compared to 61.1 per cent of male colleagues. On average, women are seven years younger than their male colleagues and have been with the organization for a shorter period. Still, the most popular jobs for women managers are personnel and marketing with the least popular being in the areas of research and development, manufacturing and production. Another finding of concern, was that younger women (those under 40) are twice as likely to resign (6 per cent) than women aged over 50 (2.8 per cent). Conversely, women over 50 are much more likely to be made redundant than their younger colleagues (IOM National Management Salary Survey 1994).

This decline in the percentage of women in management is not just confined to the British situation. Even in Australia (with its stronger Affirmative Action Policies) Still's (1993) research has revealed that Australian women's position in management within the private sector has not improved with the nine year period from 1984 to 1992 (see Table 4).

Therefore, it would seem from British and Australian evidence that rather than cracking, the glass ceiling is actually getting thicker for women in management. According to Still (1993):

In fact, considerably more women are in supervisory positions in 1992 than in 1984, while there are fewer women in all levels of management. Moreover, the marked decline in the numbers of women in junior management between 1984 and and 1992, while not so great as that for men managers, suggests that fewer will reach either middle or senior management ranks. While the reasons for this decrease are unknown, it could reflect the effects of the protracted "downsizing" of organizations in the current economic recession. However, contrary to anecdotal evidence, the recession does not seem to have impaired on middle

Table 4: Management composition of participating Australian organizations (proportion of men and women employed at each management level)

	Study 1 (1984)		Study 2 (1992)	
Management Level	Men	Women	Men	Women
Supervisors	31.8	58.3	35.4	71.0
Junior Managers	35.3	24.6	20.6	13.7
Middle Managers	21.6	14.6	33.9	14.0
Senior Managers	11.3	2.5	10.1	1.3
	100.0	100.0	100.0	100.0

Source: Still, L., (1993) p.6.

management. The 1992 figures for men are a considerable improvement over 1984, while those for women have marginally declined. It seems that women are being given less opportunity in management, despite equal opportunity and affirmative action provisions. Table 4 also suggests that the "glass ceiling" for women in senior management is not an anecdote but a fact. As far as these two studies are concerned, then, women have regressed, and not progressed, in the management ranks of these top Australian firms since 1984 (p.6–7).

If the recession and "downsizing" are not the predominant cause of the decline of women in management positions, we need to consider other possible reasons. Firstly, there are few indications that women are moving into "softer" areas of management (with supposedly more limited promotional prospects). In Australia, Still (1993) found that women have begun to move out of public relations, personnel and marketing, environmental law and scientific research (although it is not known if these new positions are still in a support or service capacity or in line management). In Britain, Nicholson and West (1988) found that female managers as a whole were more likely to be specialists. They suggested that there was a shift towards greater professionalism and specialization in management, with a reduction in the quantity of traditional management jobs. A shift which, supposedly, should create more positions for the prevalence of female management specialists!

All the evidence suggests that the two main reasons for a decline in opportunity for women managers is due to continued prejudice and discrimination from the promotional gate-keepers (predominantly male) and the fact that increasing numbers of women managers are leaving male-dominated, family-unfriendly, corporate cultures. (Marshall, in press). According to Still (1995):

> Interestingly, the majority of firms in the two studies claimed that they adopted the same criteria for the promotion of both men and women managers. Those which answered in the negative in 1984 gave women's lack of specialist job qualifications, their non-capability, separate men and women's employment areas, women's lack of locational mobility, and the administration of the organization's appraisal and development programmes as important differentiating reasons. In 1992, the negative responses were even more direct: women needed to prove themselves more than men (EEO good in theory only), some areas still restricted to males, locational mobility, appointments made without consultation (no one knows what the criteria are), and gender usually means a male candidate! (p. 8)

"Think Manager, Think Male"

Certainly, one of the major barriers facing women managers today is the continued biased attitude towards women based on the sex-role stereotyping of the managerial position. That is, the perception that the characteristics required for success as a manager are more likely to be held by men, in general, than by women in general. In other words, to "think manager, think male" (Schein, 1994).

Examining attitudes towards women managers and women in general by males is particularly important, taking into account the recent survey of 1,500 female managers and 800 male managers, carried out by the UK Institute of Management on its members (Institute of Management 1992). While 74 per cent of women "strongly agreed" that women managers brought positive skills to the workplace, only one third of men believed this to be the case. Furthermore, nearly 20 per cent of men maintained they would find it difficult to work for a woman. Their reasons included "in general, women do not make good managers – although they have much to offer in the workplace".

In the USA, Brenner *et al* (1989) and Schein et al (1989) carried out 15 year follow-up studies on the relationship between sex-role stereotypes and requisite management characteristics. These surveys revealed that, unlike women in the 1970s, American female managers and female management students today do not sex type the managerial position, but view women and men as equally likely to possess characteristics necessary for managerial success. However, American male management students viewed the management position in the same way as today's US male managers and male managers in the 1970s. All three male groups believed that, compared with women, men were more likely to possess characteristics necessary for managerial success.

More recently, Schein and Davidson (1993) were interested to discover the managerial sex typing attitudes of future managers and captains of industry in Britain. Their study used British male and female management undergraduate students (N = 379) and examined the extent to which males and females "think manager, think male" (using the Schein Descriptive Index which defines sex role stereotypes and the characteristics of successful managers). The results confirmed that "think manager, think male" is a strongly-held attitude among British undergraduate male management students. These outcomes are similar to those found among US male management students (Schein; Mueller and Jacobson 1989) and German male business students (Schein and Mueller 1992). Although the British female undergraduate management sample also sex typed the managerial position, it was to a lesser extent than their male counterparts.

An examination of the specific item ratings provided some understanding of how managerial sex typing can impact negatively on women's managerial opportunities. Characteristics such as leadership ability and skill in business matters would be considered as very important to effectiveness by most management theorists and practitioners. Yet, according to Schein and Davidson's (1993) results, women are less likely than men to possess these characteristics. If this view is held by current managers as well, it is no wonder that so many of the male managers surveyed by the Institute of Management (1992) believed that women did not make good managers. All else being equal, the perceived similarity between the characteristics of successful middle managers and men in general increases the likelihood of a male rather than a female being selected for, or promoted into, a managerial position. As such, future managers and leaders of Britain's business organizations can be expected to view women as less qualified for managerial positions, and make selection, placement and promotion decisions that impact negatively on women's advancement.

"Think Manager, Think 'Caucasian' Male" – The Plight of the Black Woman Manager
American research confirms that black and ethnic minority managers (particularly women) are doubly disadvantaged in terms of upward mobility and high levels of work/home pressures (Bell 1979; Greenhouse *et al* 1990). In addition, they are also subjected to the sex and ethnic role stereotyping of the managerial job, "think manager, think 'Caucasian' male". Indeed, according to Isles and Auluck (1991) "such findings in American studies of black managers resemble those often reported for white women managers in Britain". In the USA, the number of black employees occupying managerial positions had increased from 3.6 per cent of the national total in 1977 to 5.2 per cent in 1982, to six per cent of all managers in 1986 (Greenhouse *et al* 1990). Moreover, according to Bell (1990), ten per cent of all American black working women are now employed in executive, administrative, managerial or professional occupations.

In Britain, around five per cent of the UK population of working age are of African, Afro-Caribbean or Asian origin. Indications are that this proportion is likely to grow in the coming years and more black employees are entering managerial positions (Iles and Auluck 1991). According to Bhavnani (1994) around 70 per cent of British women aged 16–59 are economically active. For black women, the average economic activity rate is 57.6 per cent (with 76 per cent of Afro-Caribbean women being economically active compared to 61 per cent of Indian women, 29 per cent of Pakistani women and 22 per cent of Bangladesh women). This compares to a rate of 71.4 per cent for white women. However, while 56.3 per cent of white women work full-time, 69.8 per cent of black women are full-time workers. According to the most recent 1988–1990 Labour Force Survey, nine per cent of ethnic minority females in the UK are found in "Professional Manager, Employer, Employees and Managers – large establishments", compared to 11 per cent of white females (it should be noted that the high percentages of black women in the "professional" category may be misleading since this includes nursing).

To date, research addressing the issues of black managers has been almost exclusively American and the amount of total published research is according to a recent review by Cox and Nkomo (1990): "Small, relative to the importance of the topic". Indeed Bell (1990) emphasized that studies of black professional women, especially in corporate settings, are virtually excluded from the growing body of research on women in management.

Even so, from the limited studies available, what is clear is that black managers tend to be under-represented in the majority of American and British organizations, particularly at middle and higher managerial levels of the organizational hierarchy (Iles and Auluck 1991). Indications are that, like white women managers, black managers (male and female) are likely to encounter the barriers of the "glass ceiling" related to treatment discrimination. However, rather than "glass" the ceiling is more likely to be perceived as "concrete"! For example, a recent large-scale American survey of black and white male and female managers found that, compared to white managers, blacks felt less accepted in their organizations; perceived themselves as having less discretion in their jobs, received lower ratings from their supervisors on their job performance and, promotionally, were more likely to have reached career plateaux and experienced lower levels of career satisfaction (Greenhouse *et al* 1990). Bell's (1990) research has revealed that black women managers perceive themselves as living in a bi-cultural world (one culture black, the other white). Consequently, the women feel a constant "push and pull" between the different cultural contexts in their lives, which results in high stress levels particularly linked to role conflict stressors. Denton's (1990) review also emphasizes the importance of these bi-cultural role stressors and the combined effects of racism and sexism which enhance the "stressors endemic to today's cadre of black professional women". Compared to their white female counterparts, black women managers are more likely to be in token and test-case positions; be the first of their race or gender to hold a managerial position; have fewer (if any) black role models; be more likely to feel isolated and invisible; contend with stereotypical images; be more likely to experience performance pressure; and have greater home/social/work conflicts, particularly in terms of their role conflict regarding the family and the black community (Bell 1990). These findings have been replicated by Davidson (in preparation) in her exploratory study investigating the problems, pressures and barriers faced by 30 black female managers in Britain. In the words of one of her black female manager interviewees:

> You can't be yourself. You have to be a superwoman (more of a superwoman than your white female counterparts) all the time. Colleagues can come into work in jeans, but I have to dress up (even at weekends). They even remark if I have a ladder in my tights. People in the organization don't want black women to break the glass ceiling – it's lower for us than white women anyway.

Conclusion and Recommendations

Certainly, both the sex and ethnic typing of the managerial position, especially by white males, needs to be considered in the quest for parity. If women (from all ethnic groups) are to gain access to middle and upper level management positions, it seems imperative that individual, organizational and legal changes occur such that elements of the equation "think manager, think (white) male" become "think manager think qualified person" (Schein and Davidson 1993).

Corporate culture is too combined with "male values" of competition, aggression, dominance, and "transmitting" rather than "receiving" communications and needs to change to encourage negotiation, support, problem resolution, listening skills, co-operation and participation. Such change in the workplace will benefit men as well as women. Increasingly, the evidence is mounting that competition, confrontation and the "macho" management style are producing more workplace stress and less productivity (Cooper and Payne 1988). Organizations are demanding long hours and total commitment at a time when both partners are working. Corporate cultures and management styles which support and reward people, and that take into account their personal circumstances, are the ones that will survive the 1990s and beyond.

Introducing organizational policies and strategies to help break down the barriers faced by women in management such as fair selection procedures; training and job experience opportunities; career progression policies (including mentoring schemes); child-care support; adequate maternity/paternity leave, etc., are all important strategies in ensuring a healthier corporate culture. In Australia and a number of EC countries the issue of either voluntary or legislated positive action is now on the agenda. In Greece, for example, it has been suggested by the Co-ordinating Committee for Quatus that an obligatory quota of 35 per cent be introduced as a minimum target for women in senior jobs in both the public and private sectors. These issues are also being discussed actively in Belgium, Italy and Germany (Davidson and Cooper 1993). It is obvious that exposure to the US experience in this field has led many in EC countries to consider this approach, given the continuing problems that women confront not only in obtaining a job in the first instance, but also in breaking through the proverbial "glass ceiling" into senior and top management positions.

However, the recent evidence from Australia illustrates that while affirmative action policy facilitates equality of opportunity for women in management, what is also needed is emphasis on changing attitudes away from the ethos: "Think manager, think (white) male". Traditional stereotyping starts from birth and parents, the media, educational establishments and organizations, must take on the responsibility for challenging and changing attitudes that differentiate men and women. Numerous research studies have shown that both parents and teachers can transfer their own ideas about sex-role stereotypes to their children or pupils (Astin 1984; Stanworth 1986). Lecturers in Business Schools and Universities also have a responsibility to educate the future managers of tomorrow about the urgent need for fundamental changes in attitudes towards women (from all ethnic groups) and employment. (It is of interest to note that one of the undergraduate management groups in Schein and Davidson's (1993) study who had been exposed to teachings about women in management, had somewhat reduced managerial sex typing attitudes.)

In the organizational setting, research suggests that males with experience of female managers have more favourable attitudes towards them than men without such experience (Ezell *et al* 1981). Hence, increasing the numbers of women managers, particularly in senior executive positions, undoubtedly has a positive influence on male colleagues – the gatekeepers. Training should be directed to those male managers whose sex and ethnic role stereotypes are identified as most negative, and whose position in the organization may enable or hinder important career path influences. Herbert and Yost (1979) advocated these recommendations more than 15 years ago and suggested that programmes should be designed to remove the attitudinal bases for female discrimination, "to be replaced with more objective and realistic perspectives on the potential and the utilization of women as effective managers."

They went on to propose that these male managers, especially if they occupy visible and influential positions, can act as an important influence on organizational peers and subordinates in terms of attitude change. Finally, in a recent review by Lahtinen and Wilson (1994) of women and power in organizations, the authors also concluded that their main concern centres on sex-role stereotyping, most of which they believe takes place at an unconscious level and is highly influenced by the mass media. In the words of Lahtinen and Wilson (1994):

> In spite of the fact that stereotyping seems to be an unsolvable puzzle, an increased awareness of the factors leading to stereotyping will reduce barriers facing women entering managerial posts. Fortunately, stereotypical images can change, even if slowly. The main channel for changing stereotypes is the mass media: TV, magazines, and newspapers. Understanding the determinant affecting our perceptions will reduce questionable personal assessment. This understanding will be a pathway for acquiring a positive and equal stereotype of a woman in the future.

References

Astin, H S (1984). "The meaning of work in women's lives: A sociological model of career choice and work behaviour". *The Counselling Psychologist*, 12, 117–26.

Bell, E L (1990). "The bi-cultural life experience of career-orientated black women". *Journal of Organizational Behaviour*, 11(6), 459–478.

Bhavnani, R (1994). *Black Women In The Labour Market; A Research Review*. Manchester, EOC publications.

Bourantas, D and Papalexandris, N (1990). "Sex differences in leadership". *Journal of Managerial Psychology*, 5(5), 7–10.

Brennor, O C, Tomkiewicz, J and Schein, V E (1989). "The relationship between sex role stereotypes and requisite management characteristics revisited". *Academy of Management Journal*, 32, (3), 662–9.

Brett J M and Stroh, L K (1994). "Turnover of female managers" in M J Davidson and R J Burke (eds) *Women in Management: Current Research Issues*. London, Paul Chapman, 55–67.

Case, S S (1994). "Gender differences in communication and behaviour in organizations" in M J Davidson and R J Burke (eds) *Women in Management: Current Research Issues*. London, Paul Chapman, 129–43.

Commission of the European Communities (1993). *Bulletin on Women and Employment on the EC* (No 3). Brussels, EEC Pub.

Cooper, C L and Payne, R (1988) *Causes, Coping and Consequences of Stress at Work*. Chichester, John Wiley.

Cox, T and Nkomo, S M (1990). "Invisible men and women: A status report on race as a variable in organization behaviour research". *Journal of Organizational Behaviour*, II (b), 419–432.

Davidson, M J and Cooper C L (1982). *High Pressure – Working Lives of Women Managers*, London, Fontana.

Davidson, M J and Cooper C L (1983). *Stress and the Women Manager*. Oxford, Martin Robertson.

Davidson, M J and Cooper C L (1987). "Female Managers in Britain – A Comparative Review". *Human Resource Management*, 26, 217–42

Davidson, M J and Cooper, C L (1992). *Shattering the glass ceiling – The Woman Manager*. London, Paul Chapman.

Davidson, M J and Cooper, C L (eds) (1993). *European Women in Business and Management*. London, Paul Chapman.

Davidson, M J, Cooper C L and Baldini, V. "Occupational stress in female and male graduate managers – A comparative Study". *Journal of Stress Medicine*, in press.

Davidson, M J and Burke, R J (eds) (1994). *Women in Management – Current Research Issues*. London, Paul Chapman.

Denton, T C (1990). "Bonding and supportive relationships among black professional women: Rituals of restoration". *Journal of Organizational Behaviour*, 11(6), 447–458.

Devanna, M A (1987). "Women in Management: progress and promise." *Human Resource Management*, 26, 409–81.

Ezell, H F, Odewahn, C A and Sherman, J D (1981). "The effects of having been supervised by a women on perceptions of female managerial competence". *Personal Psychology*, 34, 2, 291–9.

Ferrario M (1994). "Women as managerial leaders" in M J Davidson and R J Burke (eds) *Women in Management – Current Research Issues*. London, Paul Chapman, 110–25.

Gillkes, C T (1990). "Liberated to work like dogs". Labelling black women and their work, in H Y Grossman and N L Chester (eds) *The Experience and Meaning of Work in Women's Lives*. London, Lawrence Erlbaum, 165–188.

Greenglass, E R (1995). "An interactional perspective on job related stress in managerial women". *The Southern Psychologist*, 21, 42–48.

Greenhouse, J H, Parasuraman, S and Wormley, W M (1990). "Effects on race and organizational experiences, job performance evaluations and career outcomes". *Academy of Management Journal*, 33(1), 64–86.

Helgesen, S (1990). *Female Advantage: Women's Ways of Leadership*. New York, Doubleday.

Herbert, S G and Yost, E B (1979). "Women as effective managers: A strategic model for overcoming the barriers". *Human resource Management*, 17, 18–28.

Homans, H (1987). "Man-made myths: The reality of being a woman scientist in the WHS", in Spence A and Podmore D (eds) *In a Mans World*. London, Tavistock publications, Ch 5.

Iles, P and Auluck, R (1991). "The experience of black workers", in Davidson M and Earnshaw J (eds) *Vulnerable Workers – Psychosocial and Legal Issues*. London, John Wiley, 297–322.

Instituted of Management (1992). *The Key To The Mens' Club*. Bristol, I M Books.

Lahtinen, H K and Wilson, F M (1994). "Women and power in organizations". *Executive Development*, 7 (3), 16–23.

Marshall, J (in press). "Why women leave senior management jobs: My research approach and some initial findings". in Tanton M (ed) *Women in Management: The Second Wave*. London, Routledge.

Nicholson, N and West, A (1988). *Managerial Job Change: Men and Women in Transition*. Cambridge, Cambridge University Press.

Powell, G N, "Posner, B Z and Schmidt, W H (1985). "Women: The more committed managers?" *Management Review*, 74 (6), 43–5.

Rubery, J and Fagan, C (1993). *Occupational Segregation Amongst Women and Men in the European Community*. Synthesis report, Equal Opportunities Unit V/5409/93 Brussels, Commission of the European Communities.

Stanworth, M (1986). *Gender and Schooling*. Essex, Anchor Bendon Ltd.

Still, L (1993). "Quo Vadis, Women in management?" *Women in Management Review*, 8 (3), 4–11.

Schein, V E (1989). *Sex Role Stereotyping and Requisite Management Characteristics, Past, Present and Future*. Working paper series no. WC 98–26, University of Western Ontario National Centre for Management Research & Development.

Schein, V E (1994). "Managerial sex typing: A persistent and pervasive barrier to women's opportunities", in Davidson M J and Burke R J (eds) *Women in Management – Current Research Issues*. London, Paul Chapman, 41–52.

Schein, V E and Davidson M J (1993), "Think manager, think male". *Management Development Review*, 6 (3) 24–28.

Schein, V E, Mueller, R and Jacobson, C (1989). "The relationship between sex role stereotypes and requisite management characteristics among college students", *Sex Roles*, 20, (1/2), 103–10.

Schein, V E and Mueller, R (1992). "Role stereotyping and requisite management characteristics: A cross cultural look". *Journal of Organisational Behaviour*, 13 (5) 439–47.

Webber, G (1994). BBC News and Current Affairs Publicity Press Release, Panorama Survey of Top Ten Graduate Recruiters 1983/4 using Latest Available Figures.

White, B. Cox C and Cooper, C L (1992). *Women's Career Development: A Study of High Flyers*. Oxford, Blackwell.

4

Structures, Politics, Cultures: Understanding the Gendering of Organizations[1]

Elin Kvande and Bente Rasmussen

Introduction

Organization studies as a field has been criticised for having neglected to include gender in its analyses, or, when gender is introduced, for an inadequate analysis of it (Mills 1983; Hearn and Parkin 1987). Gender in organization has until recently been treated only indirectly, either as part of Women in Management research (WIM) (Henning and Jardim 1978; Donell and Hall 1980; Marshall 1984) or as part of women and work research (Kaul and Lie 1982; Cockburn 1983, 1985, 1991; Knights and Wilmott 1986). At the same time it is fair to say that organization theory and organization research has not,

[1] Paper originally submitted to ILS Conference "100 ans de Sociologie: Petrospective, prospective" Sorbonne, Paris, 21–23 June 1993.

until recently, been addressed in feminist research. Thus organization studies need to confront the gender issue and gender studies need to put organizations on its research agenda (Kvande and Rasmussen 1990). Organizations are, after all, the area where the sex-segregation of the labour market, the unequal distribution of rewards as well as gendered cultural images and identities, are created (Acker 1990). We can now observe a move from studies focusing only on women in management to studies exploring gender in organizations. Studies are emerging where a more comprehensive understanding of gender and organization is being developed (Kvande and Rasmussen 1990; Calas and Smircich 1989, 1990; Acker 1990; Alvesson and Billing 1992). Our chapter is a contribution to this development.

Our point of departure is a research project on Norwegian male and female engineers and their career development in different work organizations. We wanted to examine opportunities for career development, graduate engineers being one of the main groups who are recruited into management positions in Norwegian industry. Between 1979 and 1985 the ratio of women at the Technical University of Norway had increased from five per cent to 25–30 per cent and has stayed there since.

These changes mirror the general changes in women's relation to work and their participation in society in general in Norway where 75 per cent of women work and 60 per cent of them work full-time.

We will develop our understanding of gender in organizations in a dialogue with this empirical material. In this dialogue we will use two strands of theorizing. One strand concerns the different ways of understanding and analyzing gender that have been developed in feminist research (Harding 1986; Calas and Smircich 1989). The other strand involves the different theories that have been developed in organization studies. By combining the two strands we will show how this "marriage" between feminist theories and organization theories enables us to develop a differentiated understanding of gender in organization.

From Women in Management to Women in Organizations
The main field in research aimed at understanding women in
organizations has been the Women in Management (WIM)
literature which was mainly developed from the mid-seventies
in the USA. A common trait of the WIM literature is the focus
on individual characteristics of women, in the light of sex
socialization and gender roles (Donell and Hall 1980; Powell
1989). Research on women in management, such as female
graduate engineers, mainly uses a sex role model approach
attaching importance to socialization. In such research much
emphasis has been put on women's lack of self-confidence and
ambition in order to answer the "why so few" question, which
is the typical research question in this tradition (Terborg
1977a; Donell and Hall 1980). We have structured the studies
in this research tradition in the following four categories:

- the "trait" approach, where the main emphasis is whether
  women are "suited" to management
- the "motivation" approach, with the focus on women's
  "lack of" self-confidence or motivation
- the "strategy" approach, where the emphasis is on whether
  or not women are good enough strategists, making use of the
  right informal channels
- the "choice" approach, showing that women choose to give
  priority to their home and family rather than a career.

The "trait" approach, is part of an Anglo-American tradition
of research where certain *characteristics* of managers are seen as
an important element of leadership theory (Yukl 1981). It is
used as a basis for evaluating how far women "are suited" to
leadership or whether they represent "deviant" values opposed
to the traditional norms and values associated with management (Bartol 1978; Donell and Hall 1980). Terborg (1977b)
says of the studies in the trait condition: "In general women are
perceived as being dependent, passive and subjective, and as
lacking such attributes as competitiveness, ambition and
leadership abilities".
    The "motivation" approach is based on the idea that women

uphold traditional women's jobs because they lack motivation and self-confidence; they score lower than men on these variables (Terborg 1977b; Hackett and Betz 1981). According to this view, women will try to avoid success because it can have negative consequences, such as loss of femininity and social recognition. They have a fear of success (Horner 1972). However, later research indicates that the so-called "motivation" reflects cultural stereotypes of male and female areas of achievement and of work (Nieva and Gutek 1981). Hackett and Betz (1981) maintain that it is natural to assume that women's work expectations will be lower than men's in a number of areas because women's chances have been and still are very poor in many areas.

In the "strategy" tradition, Henning and Jardim (1978) in their book "The Managerial Women" are the main representatives. According to Henning and Jardim, men and women have different ideas of the concept of "career". Women define career in terms of personal growth and self-realization. Men are more likely to see career as a series of jobs leading upwards providing status and recognition. Because of these different concepts, women are not aware of the informal network of connections which men have and use in their careers. This "hidden" system has a great deal of influence on the way work is organized, and until women learn to use it as men do they will be starting with a serious "handicap" in their way to the top, according to this view.

The "choice" approach emphasizes women's choice or giving priority to home and family as the explanation of why there are so few women in non-traditional jobs and in management, and this is the predominant approach of the four. It is supported by studies showing that relatively few of the women who make a career in public or private business are married compared to the corresponding group of men (Hemes 1982). This is stressed particularly in surveys among American women in management positions (Henning and Jardim 1978; Business Week 1987). However, research from USA and the UK indicates that women in top positions now are integrating the role of mother with that of manager (Epstein 1983;

Marshall 1984). A number of research reports have appeared pointing out that there may well be many advantages for married working women over the unmarried ones (Reskin 1978; Lukkonen-Groow and Stolte Heiskanen 1983; Marshall 1984; Kvande and Rasmussen 1990).

A common denominator of the four categories presented is that they refer to characteristics of the individual rather than factors related to the work-conditions offered to men and women by the organizations where they work. The alternative to this individual focus is to attach more importance to structural conditions in the organizations where women work than to individual characteristics of women (Acker and Van Houten 1974; Kanter 1977; Epstein 1981; Kvande and Rasmussen 1989, 1990).

An example of such an approach is given by Rosabeth Moss Kanter (1977). She shows how the structural conditions in a large corporation limit women's opportunities. Kanter's approach must be read as a criticism of individual-oriented explanations. Women's positions in the labour market are on the lower levels of the corporate hierarchy with limited opportunities for mobility. According to Kanter (1977), it is therefore unreasonable to conclude that women limit their career aspirations because of their sex-roles or family. She presents an alternative structural model which involves the structure of opportunity (meaning the challenges available, the chances of learning new skills and the earning of organizational rewards), the power (i.e. ability to get things done), and the social composition of groups (here meaning the relative number of women in work groups and departments).

The third structural variable, the social composition of groups, is considered to be her most original contribution. There she focuses on the importance of the relative number of representatives of different social groups in a workplace. The situation is very different if there is only one woman, some women, a minority group of reasonable size or a balanced group of men and women. If women are alone or only in a small minority, they will be seen by the majority as "tokens" or symbols of their group and not as individuals (Kanter 1977).

Kanter has been criticized for the gender-neutrality implied in the relative number position (Fairhurst and Snavely 1983; Ott 1989; Kvande and Rasmussen 1990). Our main critique of Kanter, however, is that she studied only one company, with a traditional hierarchical structure. Therefore she does not take into account that different types of organizations may involve different structures of opportunity for the employees. Like most organization researchers she understands the bureaucratic and hierarchical structure of organizations as *the* structure of "modern" organizations (Clegg 1990).

Kanter represents a move from the traditional management research in organization studies as she focuses on organization members at many levels, and our structural perspective is inspired by this as well as by the Scandinavian sociotechnical work research in the work-democracy tradition (Emery and Thorsrud 1969; Herbst 1976). In this tradition we are especially interested in alternatives to hierarchies and in variations in organizational structures in order to test the hypothesis that organizations vary in opportunity structures.

Method
Our structural approach to male and female graduate engineers' careers and development led us to choose a qualitative method in our study. We needed information about the structural conditions of the organizations, the individual characteristics of the engineers and the processes of gender differentiation within the organizations. With these needs in mind three different data-sets were employed.

First, case studies were carried out of six large Norwegian companies that employed many graduate engineers, and more than ten female graduate engineers. By choosing organizations with different types of ownership (public and private); within different industries (chemical, electronics, oil, construction, research and development); with different employment requirements and policies towards women, we wanted to focus on different structural conditions. It was considered that these variations would also make an analytical or substantial generalization possible (Yin 1984).

Within each of the firms we carried out in-depth interviews with *pairs* of graduate engineers: one male and one female engineer who graduated the same year and were employed within the same department. Through our selection of pairs from the different firms we could compare men and women across the firms and within the firms. We made in-depth interviews with 26 pairs of graduate engineers in the six companies. We also interviewed the managers of the pairs and key informants about market, organization and personnel policy.

Secondly, we carried out a postal survey of all female members of the Norwegian Engineering Society, asking questions about their work and work experience, career and career plans, management, family and housework.

The third and final data set comprised a national survey with structured questions of all groups of female academics concentrating on the themes of work and family. From this data set we selected the responses from women educated at the Technical University.

Our study is reported in a book that discusses all our findings around work, careers, family and individual strategies and differences among women and men. In this article we will draw mainly upon the six case studies. We will, however, also use some of our findings from the two surveys.

Different Organizations – Different Opportunities
The inadequacy of a single explanation for women's lack of participation in management was confirmed in our study. Our surveys showed that the female graduate engineers were motivated for careers without sacrificing a family. When asked whether or not they would take a management position when offered, 70 per cent of them said that they would. The highest motivation we found among the mothers of one child (82 per cent), and the lowest among the mothers of three or more children (63 per cent). We also found that the female graduate engineers were more often married and had more children than Norwegian women in general. The female graduate engineers

wanted to combine family and career (Kvande and Rasmussen 1990, Chapter 5).

Studying *different* types of organizations turned out to be very important in our study of female graduate engineers. We had expected to find that the women had the same, equally unfavourable, opportunities in all the firms. However, we found that there were greater variations between the employees in different firms than between the male and female graduate engineers in our sample as a whole. We found that the six companies could be divided into two main groups. Two of the companies showed no systematic differences in opportunities for career and development between male and female graduate engineers. The other four showed a traditional pattern of gendered differences in opportunities: the male engineers had systematically better opportunities than their comparable female colleagues.

There are some striking differences in organizational structure between the "equal opportunity" companies and the others. We have isolated characteristics of the two different types of organization in order to study them as ideal types. These ideal types serve as a reference point against which the individual companies can be measured. The companies where we find that men have systematically better opportunities than women, are characterized by a hierarchical organization structure operating with stable markets. The companies where opportunities do not vary systematically according to gender are characterized by a less hierarchical and more flexible network-type of organization and they operate within turbulent and changing markets. We labelled the two types *static hierarchies* and *dynamic networks*. The dynamic networks we found in the telecommunications and electronics industry and in engineering (construction of oil installations). The static hierarchies we found in an oil company, the chemical industry, research and development and public telecommunications.

By looking at variations in organizational structure we take a step further than former studies of women and organizations where the hierarchical bureaucracy organization has been treated as the dominant modern organization (Kanter 1977;

Ferguson 1984; Ressner 1986). Thereby the researchers have been able to maintain the view that organization structures are gender-neutral and that the gendering occurs through a separate structure or process, like partriarchy, as Acker notes (Acker 1989). Our results show how different organization structures are gendered differently.

Our results do not confirm the common belief in the social democratic Scandinavian cultures, that public organizations further women's careers whereas private organizations do not. This belief is built mainly upon a Weberian logic that within public bureaucracies the impersonal rules and regulations will hinder discrimination and arbitrary treatment of women. In private organizations the subjective views of (male) managers are supposed to exclude women from important jobs and positions. This belief in the objective functioning of rules and regulations in organizations has been a cornerstone of the equal opportunity policy in the Scandinavian societies (Hernes 1982). Our results seriously challenge this belief.

We shall explain the differences in opportunities for men and women in the two types of organizations by discussing some of their characteristics. Dynamic networks are open to innovation and change whereas static hierarchies are status quo organizations. The dynamic networks make women visible as professionals and provide leadership training whereas the static hierarchies make women invisible as professionals and promote homosocial reproduction in management. These characteristics are discussed in turn below.

Dynamic Networks
We found that the organizations with no systematic differences in opportunities between male and female graduate engineers were the ones where the market was turbulent and required an organization structure which was very flexible and open towards new approaches. These companies have had to be dynamic; they have profited from trying out new ideas and non-traditional approaches. This in turn has created a corporate culture which welcomes change and new ways of doing things, including trying out women in non-traditional

positions. They have a fundamental openness towards change. The hard competition forces them to use all their resources. One of the women in a dynamic network organization said: "I'm surprised at the opportunities we have here. There is room for new ways of thinking in the organization. It doesn't have a fixed structure but has to keep alert and be innovative all the time and has to follow the signs of the times. I think this is what makes it more open to taking on women and giving us opportunities".

The power structure in network organizations strengthens the dynamic aspect. The decentralized structure is based on the idea that everyone who has relevant knowledge for the problem in question is involved in decision-making. Different ways of thinking, values and opinions represent a resource for interpreting signals from the market and the environment and in working out solutions to new challenges. Women and their points of view are seen as a resource for the organization.

In dynamic networks the work is organized in teams where all members are equally important and all contribute knowledge and effort on an equal basis. As they work, the graduate engineers get to know each other's academic and personal qualifications. The women become visible as professionals to their colleagues and superiors.

The organization of tasks is flexible in the dynamic networks. The employees here do not have clearly defined tasks and areas of responsibility, but their tasks and responsibility alter progressively as the situation changes. The employees are given responsibility and challenges whether they want them or not. One of the women stated: "What I don't like is never having time enough to follow up all the challenges in the job, at least not in a normal working day". A female manager told us how she solved the pressure between having a family and a demanding job: "I am known as one who uses flexitime in the extreme. I have done it the way I want, and it has been accepted. Maximum flexitime is an important condition in my life. The kids decide the tempo in the morning. When I get to my job, I work hard. I like it that way".

In dynamic networks the engineers get a gradual training for leadership through their work, and this seems to suit women well. It also makes it easier for women to volunteer for new tasks. Managerial careers in dynamic networks tend to follow "natural routes where the position in a direct result of the tasks and responsibility one has had beforehand". (See also Kanter 1984, 1989).

The function of the manager in the dynamic network is to be a co-ordinator of a team. When decisions are made, in close consultation with all those involved and all available experts on the topic, it is important for the manager to be able to delegate, to co-operate with colleagues and to inspire them. These are the very qualities that women feel are particularly important in the managerial position, and this is where they think that they, as women, have something to offer as managers.

These findings correspond to the studies of organizations and innovation, where both Burns and Stalker (1961) and Kanter (1984) find similar differences between the stable, and the changing and innovative organizations, and situate us within the contingency school of organization theory (Burns and Stalker 1961; Lawrence and Lorsch 1967; Pfeffer and Salancik 1978). However, gender has not previously been brought into the analysis of the structure of organizations and their environment. We find that the gendering of organizations is influenced by the characteristics of the environment and by the structures that they develop to suit this content.

Static Hierarchies

The other group of companies we have labelled static. This is because they operate in very stable markets with few if any requirements to change. The centralized pyramid structure of the static hierarchy ensures a continual reproduction of the culture, which makes such organizations very stable. The organization will try to maintain the status quo in order to avoid disturbances. Therefore, it is not open to change or ready to accept anything new or different. A frustrated man said: "The responsibility for change lies with the managers, and they do not always welcome initiatives from below. We send proposals for new methods or new products the formal right way, but don't get a response. We, who receive the signals, are not allowed to follow them up, and the ones who are responsible for following up, are not in the position to understand the signals".

In organizations dominated by men, women represent something new and different and will therefore tend to be met with rejection or scepticism. Women are, or are assumed to be, different from men and therefore they have problems being considered relevant and central to the organization. Women are allowed to do traditional women's work in women's jobs, such as office or secretarial work where they are subordinated to men in a "natural" way in these organizations. If, on the other hand, women impinge on areas dominated by men, such as technical work and managerial positions, they challenge the existing gender arrangement and hence the stability of the organization. A newly-appointed female manager of a department told us: "I did not get this position without a struggle. There were some old men in the department, and they had their crown princes. Because I knew that, I contacted the union representative when the job was announced. I applied, and I went to the National Board of Equal Opportunity, when I was surpassed. The old men were very angry when they had to give me the job after all".

In the static hierarchies we find all the well-known mechanisms described by Kanter and others (Kanter 1977). Women become invisible as professionals and get stuck in blind alleys. A young woman in a static hierarchy told us: "I never get any feedback on my performance. When I prepare a paper, my boss never tells me that it is OK, or suggests any changes. The only thing he ever said when I asked him once, was that my handwriting was very nice. I manage in this job because I can bring work home with me and discuss it with my husband".

A career in a hierarchy involves promotion to a higher position. To get new challenges, new tasks and increased responsibility in a hierarchical organization, you apply for another job, either in a different department or upwards in your own department. A woman's chances of getting a better job are poor because they depend on whether she has been *visible* as a capable and important member of the organization. In order to become visible she must have had challenges, met them successfully and shown her superiors that she was professionally outstanding. In hierarchial organizations, a woman is professionally *invisible* and this puts her in the back of the row for more important jobs.

Other research has shown that managers choose managers who are similar to themselves, that is with the same educational background, the same social background and the same sex and race (Mills 1963; Kanter 1977). Managers recruit new managers who will fill their posts in the way that they themselves want them to be filled so that the systems will continue to function well. Anyone who is similar to the manager is assumed to think the same way as he does and to make similar decisions. Women are different from men and in some ways behave differently. Men who are similar to their managers and follow the same norms and values can make themselves noticed as supporters of the managers and be visible. This gives them the best chance of promotion. This homosocial reproduction at managerial level reinforces the re-production of the status quo and thereby male domination.

We had chosen companies with and without programmes for affirmative action for women. One might expect that the firms with affirmative action would be the ones with good opportunities for women. This was not the case. The dynamic networks did not have affirmative action programmes. Some of the static hierarchies did. The affirmative action we found was typically not directed at the organization structure but at the motivation of individual women. This strengthens our point about the importance of focusing on organizational structure and not on the traits or motivation of individual women in order to understand women's careers.

Women's Opportunities in Changing Organizations
According to our findings, de-hierarchization becomes an important measure to increase women's opportunities. Recent studies of organizational change and structure of organizations

(Piore and Sabel 1984; Hand 1984; Kern and Schumann 1984; Kanter 1978; Clegg 1990) focus upon a trend towards such de-hierarchization or de-differentiation as we have found in the dynamic networks.

Rosabeth Moss Kanter's more recent work on big corporations in North America and Europe (Kanter 1989) suggests that these companies are moving away from diversification towards maximizing their core business competence. They develop by delayering the hierarchy and making the company leaner. The borders between the company and its surroundings also change through strategic alliances with other companies, sub-contractors and spin-offs from the old mother-firm. They try to strengthen their relations to their customers and to their business partners through alliances. Kanter describes these firms as post-bureaucratic or post-entrepreneurial because they try to combine the strength and stability of a big corporation with the agility and innovative capacity of the entrepreneur. The reasons for these changes are the changes in market conditions and increased competition.

Stewart R Clegg (1990) uses studies of new organizational forms especially in Asian industrialized countries, but also in French, Italian and Swedish industry, to advocate the decline of modernist organizational principles based on a differentiation of tasks, familiar in Tayloristic and bureaucratic organizations. Clegg sees many examples of organizations that are highly competitive but are not conforming to these principles. He sees tendencies to de-differentiation and de-hierarchization which he labels as the emerging postmodern organizations (Clegg 1990).

If these tendencies are dominant, we could expect that women's opportunities are changing for the better. However, although the dynamic organizations may give women good opportunities for career and development and equal opportunities with their male colleagues, that does not mean that they are de-gendered or gender neutral. Dynamic networks will make use of women to further *their* ends, and they will use the women to the point of exploitation if they are allowed. They are based on the male principle of work orientation: "The job should be foremost in your life, and the family should accommodate to job demands". They may be flexible and you may do the job wherever or whenever you want, as long as it is ready on time. The female graduate engineers use this flexibility to juggle their job and family responsibilities in co-operation with their spouses. Only as long as women are willing to conform to this traditional male work-ethic are they given opportunities.

It is also a fact that gender and sex still play a role for the women in the organization, even if they may have career opportunities or management positions. They may encounter sexual harassment in the workplace. Male colleagues at the same level, or at a lower level, are still likely to have problems with women in authority. A female manager in a dynamic organization reported on how she felt she had to downplay her managerial authority towards a colleague who had been a competitor for her position. She felt responsible for his dignity and felt that she had to treat him as an equal even though she was now his boss. Thus "equal opportunity" organizations will still be gendered (Acker 1990). This brings us to an explicit discussion on how to understand gender.

Gender and Organization – Reconceptualization
Traditionally, gender has been treated more or less as a dichotomous variable: as the difference between two cate-gories – men and women. This concept of gender as "difference" and a dichotomous variable has been challenged by feminist researchers. Black feminists and feminists from the third world challenged the concept of a woman's perspective that was supposed to include the interests of all women (Spellman 1988; Aphteker 1989; Collins 1990). Changes in women's lives also made it problematic to use a general concept of woman. Women became diversified through their entrance into the world of work at different places, times and social levels. This has made a differentiation in the understanding of women necessary. Male and female and masculinities and femininities were introduced instead of the clear dichotomous concepts of man and woman. The focus moved from the differences between

men and women to the meaning of gender in different situations and contexts. Gender becomes a perspective from which society is understood as gender-constructed. This becomes a lens for analysing the gendering of seemingly gender-neutral phenomena.

In the course of the 80s the concept of gender or the gender system was developed (Harding 1986; Hirdman 1988). The gender system is used to refer to structural, relational and symbolic differentiation between men and women. Rather than asking how female oppression is produced and maintained as in the theories on patriarchy (Hartmann 1979), the question is how gender is an integrated part of processes and structures which have hitherto been considered gender neutral.

Theories on gender system make it possible to visualise male dominance and female suppression as being made up of a great many and different components and processes. Hirdman (1988) characterizes the gender system by two logics: dichotomy, dividing society into male and female areas, and hierarchy, with the male as the normal and universally valid form and the female as deviant and subordinated. She understands the segregation of male and female as something that is happening continuously through processes that create meaning and dominance. Human beings become men and women through cultural transmission, integration into social institutions and socialization.

Acker (1990) proposes a similar gender perspective for studies of organizations. She understands organizations as basically characterized by gender and gender arrangement, that is the male domination, of the society. Gendering is not an addition to other structures or processes that are gender neutral. It is part of these processes and they cannot be understood without analysing gender.

Gendering in organizations occurs in at least five interacting processes (Acker 1990). These processes are:

- construction of divisions along lines of gender: division of labour, allowed behaviours, power and the means of maintaining the divisions in the structures of the labour market, the family and the state

- construction of symbols that explain, express, reinforce or oppose those divisions. These can take many forms: in language, ideology or dress
- patterns of interaction between men and women, women and women, men and men, including all those patterns that enact dominance and submission
- gendered components of individual identity, which may include consciousness of the existence of the other three aspects of gender
- gender is implicated in the fundamental ongoing of creating and conceptualising social structures. Gender is a constitutive element in organizational logic as well as in the construction of class.

This gender perspective opens up the possibility that differences between men and women may not necessarily be hierarchic, that is dominated by men. We consider that this perspective makes it possible to see ruptures in the general oppression or subordination of women. It indicates a possibility that even within a general male dominated society we may find situations without female subordination, that is gender differences without hierarchy. Within this perspective we can understand our findings in some organizations offering women the same opportunities for careers as men.

In the following section we will show how gender in organizations can be understood as an integrated part of political and cultural processes in organizations. This indicates a move from a predominantly structural perspective to a perspective where we combine the structural with political and cultural traditions.

Organizations as Gender-Political Systems
Thus far in the analysis of the empirical findings of this paper, we have had to differentiate between organizations to understand the conditions under which women are given good opportunities. If we had stopped with the structural perspective, we would have treated organizational structures as gender neutral and gender as a dichotomous variable. We will now

analyse the organizations as political systems, as the arena for power, conflicts and interests (Morgan 1987), and we take this one step further by introducing the term gender-political system.

Burns (1961) shows that modern organizations promote forms of political behaviour because they are systems *simultaneously* involving co-operation and competition. These conflicting dimensions are clearly symbolized in the hierarchical map of organizations which is both a system for co-operation, a rational sharing of the tasks, and a career ladder to motivate individuals to upward mobility. As there are fewer positions the higher one gets in the hieararchy there is progressively more competition. In our study we found that one of the great differences between the two types of organizations was the multiple challenges in the dynamic networks compared to the very limited career openings in the static hierarchies.

In the hierarchical organizations, women have to compete with men for limited organizational rewards such as promotion and opportunities to influence decisions (Harlan and Weiss 1980). This competition makes the conflicting interests, the unequal power and the possible disputes between men and women within the organization visible. In a gender perspective it becomes clear that the conflicts, power and interests within an organization also include what men and women are allowed to do, how they are allowed to behave and how men and women are to be ranked and valued. This is one of the main gendering processes in the construction of the gender-political system in organizations. We found that especially within the static hierarchies the competition between men and women for opportunities was a problem for the female engineers. Their male competitors made gender an issue to exclude women in an occupation that has traditionally been totally male-dominated and in an organizational structure where women are made invisible as professionals this was not very difficult. We have in our analysis of the two types of organizations put much emphasis on a structural explanation pointing to the differences in structures between hierarchies and networks in our analysis of the two types of organizations as gender-political systems. By labelling them static hierarchies and dynamic networks, however, we have also pointed to the close connection between the organization's culture and its structure. The general climate in dynamic networks is positive towards women because of the openness towards new ideas and approaches, while in the static hierarchies women are seen as "foreigners" or intruders because they are different and may threaten the status quo. Gender is an integral element in both the structure and the culture of the organizations, and we will therefore advocate an approach that does not separate structure and culture, but sees them as two interlinked aspects.

In our analysis of the two different types of organizations, we found that they were gendered in very different ways; they produce different gendering processes. By introducing gendering processes in organizations, we also introduce the "actors" within the organizational structures. We can understand static hierarchies and dynamic networks as organizations with different gendering processes. The two types of organizations with their different organizational structures become arenas for different types of organizational actors, or stages where different types of organizational actors can play the leading part. The two types of organizational structures make room for different types of men and women, different masculinities and different femininities, "placing some men and women in the foreground and others in the background".

We will develop our analysis of the two different types of organization further by using more of the data from the case studies and some of the data from the surveys. We will especially present data on the differences between the women and the differences between the men to understand which types of men and women, or masculinities and femininities, will have opportunities in the two types of organizations.

According to this way of analysing the organizations, the static hierarchy can be seen as a stable patriarchial organization in the traditional sense of the word, where the older men rule over the younger ones. The rules of the game are old and well-known, and the younger men are disciplined by the competition for careers and possibilities that the elder can bestow upon them. Women are in principle non-persons in these organizations. It is primarily a question of fathers and sons or kings and crown princes, not of daughters or princesses. Dynamic networks are organizations in change without the same stable power structure. This gives the younger (and dynamic) men – and in our case also crucially young dynamic women in the organization – opportunities for development, career, influence and power. Dynamic networks suit the young professionals who want to expose themselves now and not in the far future and do not want to be subordinates of the older men, that is controlled by them.

In these days, it is "in" to make room for women in organizations, at least, in Scandinavia and in the USA. A totally male-dominated organization is no longer legitimate in Norway. "Modern" organizations therefore can be seen to promote women's opportunities, at least in words. Dynamic organizations are examples of modern and innovative organizations. They give room for women, at least for those women who participate according to the same principles as the young and dynamic men. Many of the female graduate engineers do; they want a career as well as a family, and they want to show what they can do.

The dynamic network may therefore well be the organization for the dynamic men and the "new" women whereas the static hierarchy is the organization for the older men and their subordinate and loyal crown princes. Female graduate engineers as a group are typical representatives of the "new" women: women who choose professions and careers like men do and who do not accept a traditional female role in a sub-ordinated position at work. We have seen that the female graduate engineers had better opportunities in dynamic net-works than in static hierarchies. If we look more closely at the women in our study who have made a career and reached middle management positions, they are mainly from a category of women that we in our book have named "the challengers" (Kvande and Rasmussen 1990, Chapter 11). They are women who have chosen both a career and a family and who create a managerial role in their own way; different from most of their male colleagues. They are *female* managers. The more detailed analysis in our book also suggests that the challengers are typically their father's daughters: they are daughters of graduate engineers, most of them managers. They have fathers who have motivated them and supported them in choosing a non-traditional education and profession like engineering. Therefore they come equipped with both the technical interest and also the class-background that give them confidence and strength when they go into the male-dominated profession.

To refer to opportunities for female graduate engineers in the dynamic organizations is not necessarily to say anything about the opportunities for other women in the same type of organization. It may say something about the opportunities for the women who are "more like men" in their attitude to work, who want to participate in working life like men who do not accept a subordinate position or show traditional female attitudes. The situation may well be different for other women and for women at lower levels of the organization.

If we combine a political and a cultural perspective, organizations can be understood as arenas where multiple cultures and countercultures compete to define the nature of situations. The corporate culture can then be understood as a result of political processes where different groups with different interests compete (Frost 1987; Meek 1988; Knights and Wilmott 1991; Knights and Morgan 1990). Gender identity, like different masculinities and femininities, is an important element in these processes.

Morgan and Knights (1990) use this perspective in their analysis of how jobs become gendered. Using a case from the banking and insurance sector, they describe how the aggressive male sales culture met with resistance from the male bank hierarchy. The bankers represented a masculinity that was very different from the masculinity of the sales representatives. The bankers were paternalistic, steady, responsible and cautious whereas the sales reps were aggressive, high-performing and had to have "nerve" and "a bit of cheek" to persuade the public to buy their product. The bankers allied with the female staff at the counter to get rid of the sales reps from the insurance company in the bank so that the female clerks could take over the selling of life insurance. Morgan and Knights show how these discussions about the gender of jobs took place as a discussion about the bank's strategy (Morgan and Knights 1990).

We will suggest that when the female graduate engineers have good opportunities in dynamic organizations, it is because they match the dominant male group (the young "dynamic" men) in the company in their views on work and organization and in their opposition to the traditional male hierarchical rule. They "find" each other in their interests in getting something done in different ways, by alternative means. In Morgan and Knights' case, we also see alliances between a dominant male group and a group of women against another and threatening male group leading to new opportunities for women. It may seem that the alliances between groups of men and groups of women is crucial if you want to understand the opportunities for women at work, and in these alliances the gendered work identities play an important role.

Conclusion
We started out by underlining the necessity for organizational studies to confront the gender issue and for feminist research to acquire a better understanding of organizations. We also advocated a more differentiated approach to the issue of gender and organization where both women and men as well as organizations were seen as heterogeneous. In the first part of this chapter, we have illustrated the importance of a differentiated view of organizations by choosing a research design which addressed variation in organizational structures.

The focus of variations in organizational structure was selected as an alternative approach both to the dominant Women in Management literature where the focus has mainly been on women's individual traits, as well as an alternative to Rosabeth Moss Kanter's structural approach which included only one type of organization (Kanter 1977). This perspective would seem to be of great importance when studying female graduate engineers and their opportunities for development and careers. We found that the opportunities for career and development for women vary according to the organizational structure of the company (or team). In static organizations with hierarchical structure the women have poor opportunities whereas in the dynamic organizations with a teamwork and network structure they have good opportunities. These findings were discussed in light of new organization studies showing a development of de-hierarchization towards leaner and more flexible organizations (Kanter 1989; Clegg 1990).

As a second stage, we have combined our empirical results with two strands of theorizing. We used elements from feminist theory on the understanding of gender and combined this with political systems theory and a cultural understanding of organizations. This enabled us to illustrate how to avoid analysing organizational structures as gender-neutral and show how gender is an integrated part of political and cultural processes in organizations. The differentiation in the category of women and the category of men enabled us to analyse the organizations as the arena for different gendered identities, different masculinities and different femininities.

References

Acker, J (1989). "The Problem with Patriarchy". *Sociology*. *vol. 23*, no. 2.

Acker, J (1990). "Hierarchies, Jobs, Bodies: A theory of gendered organizations". *Gender & Society, vol. 4.*, No. 2.

Acker, J and Van Houten, D (1974). "Differential Recruitment and Control: The Sex Structuring of Organizations". *Administrative Science Quarterly, 19.*

Aptheker, B (1989). *Tapestries of Life. Women's Work Women's Consciousness and the Meaning of Daily Life.* Amherst, University of Massachusetts Press,

Bartol, K M (1978). "Sex Structuring of organizations: a search for possible causes". *Academy of Management Review*, no. 3.

Burns, T (1961). "Mechanisms of Organizational Change". *Administrative Science Quarterly, 6.*

Burns, T and Stalker, G M (1961). *The Management of Innovation*, London, Tavistock,

Business Week, 1987, June 22.

Calas, M and Smircich, L (1989). "Using the 'F' word: Feminist theories and the social consequences of organizational research". Paper presented at the August *Academy of Management Meeting*, Washington.

Clegg, S R (1990). *Modern organizations. Organization Studies in the Postmodern World.* London, Sage.

Cockburn, C (1983). *Brothers*, London, Pluto

Cockburn, C (1985). *Machinery of Dominance*, London, Pluto.

Cockburn, C (1991). *In the way of women*, Basingstoke, Macmillan.

Collins, P H (1990). *Black feminist Thought: Knowledge, Consciousness, and the politics of Enlightenment.* Boston, Unwin Hyman.

Deal, T E and Kennedy, A (1982). *Corporate Cultures*, Reading, Mass. Addison Wesley.

Donnel, S and Hall, J (1980). "Men and Women as Managers: A significant case of no significant difference", *Organizational Dynamics*, Spring.

Epstein, C F (1983). *Women in Law*, New York, Basic Books.

Fairhurst, G og Snavely, K (1983). "Majority and Token Minority Group Relationships: Power Acquisitional Communication", *Academy of Management Review*, no. 8(1).

Ferguson, K (1984). *The feminist case against bureaucracy*, Philadelphia, Temple University Press.

Hackett, G and Betz, N E A (1981). "A self-efficacy approach to the career development of women." *Journal of Vocational Behaviour*, no. 18.

Handy, C (1984). *The future of Work*, Oxford, Basil Blackwell.

Harding, S (1986). *The Science Question in Feminism.* Milton Keynes, Open University Press.

Harlan, A and Weiss, C (1980). *Women in Managerial Careers: Third Progress Report*, Wesley, Mass, Wesley Centre for Research on Women.

Hartmann, H "The unhappy marriage of marxism and feminism. Towards a more progressive union." *Capital & Class*, vol. 70, no. 416.

Hearn, J and Parkin, W (1987). *Sex at work. The Power and the Paradox of organization sexuality* Brighton, Wheatsheaf.

Henning, M and Jardim, A (1978). *The Managerial Woman*, London, Marion Boyars.

Herbst, P (1976). *Alternative to hierarchy*. The Hague, Nijhoff.

Hernes, H M (1982). *Staten – kvinner inqen adqang?* Oslo, Universitetsforlaget.

Hirdman, Y (1988). Genussystemet – reflexioner krlng kvinnors sociala underordning *M: Kvinnovetenskaplia Tidsskrifl.* no. 3.

Horne, M (1972). "Toward an understanding of achievement-related conflicts in women," *Journal of Social Issues*, no. 28.

Kanter, R M (1977). *Men and Women of the Corporation*. New York, Basic Books.

Kanter, R M (1984). *The Change Masters*. London, Allen & Unwin.

Kanter, R M (1989). *When Giants Learn to Dance*. London, Simon and Schuster.

Kaul, H and Lie, M (1982). "When paths are vicious circles –How women's working conditions limit influence", *Economic and Industrial Democracy*, 3, no. 4.

Kern, H and Schumann, M (1984). "Das ende der arbeitsteiluna. Rahonalisieruna" in der *industriellen Produktion*. Munchen:

Knights, D and Morgan, G (1991). "Corporate strategy, organizations and subjectivity: A critique". *Organization Studies*, v 1.12, no. 2.

Knights, D and Wilmott, H (1986). *Gender and the labour process*. Aldershot, Gower.

Knights, D and Wilmott, H (1991). "Power and subjectivity at work: From degradation to subjugation in social relations". *Sociology*, no. 4.

Kvande, E and Rasmussen, B (1990). *Nve kvinneliv. Kvinner i menns oraanisasioner* Oslo, Ad Notam.

Lawrence, P and Lorsch, J (1967). *Organization and Environment*. Boston, Harvard Business School.

Lukkonen, G and Stolte-Heiskanen, V (1983). "Myths and Realities of Role Incompatibility of Women Scientists", *Acta Sociologica, Vol. 26.*

Marshall, J (1984). *Women Managers – Travellers in a male world.* Chichester, Wiley.

Meek, V L (1988). "Organizational Culture: Origins and weaknesses". *Organization Studies.* vol. 9, no. 4.

Mills, A (1983). "Organization, gender and culture". *Organization Studies*, no. 3.

Mills, C W (1963). "The American Business Elite: A Collective Portrait". In Horowitz, I L (ed.) *Power, Politics and People.* New York, Ballantine.

Morgan, G and Knights, D (1990). "Gendering Jobs: Corporate strategy, managerial control and the dynamics of job segregation". *Work, Employment & Society.*

Nieva U and Gutek, B A (1981). *Women and Work*, New York, Praeger Publ.

Ott, M (1989). "Effects of the Male-Female Ratio at Work Policewomen and Male Nurses", *Psychology of Women Quarterly*, no. 1.

Peters, T J and Waterman, R H (1982). *In Search of Excellence: Lessons from America's Best-Run Corporations.* New York, Harper & Row.

Pfeffer, J (1977). "The Ambiguity of Leadership". *Academy of Management Review*, vol. 2.

Pfeffer, J and Salancik, G R (1978). "The External Control of Organizations". *A Resource Dependence Perspective* New York, Harper & Row.

Piore, M J and Sabel, C F (1984). *The second industrial divide: Prospects for prosperity.* New York, Basic Books.

Powell, G N (1988). *Women and Men in Management.* Newbury Park, Ca., Sage.

Reskin, B F (1978). "Sex Differentiation and The Social Organization of Science". In Gaston, J *The Sociology of Science*, San Francisco.

Ressner, U (1986). *The hidden hierarchy.* London, Gower

Spellman, E (1988). *Inessential Woman.* Boston, Beacon Press.

Terborg, J (1977). (a) "Women in Management"; a Research Review. *Journal of Applied Psychology* no. 6.

Terborg, J R (1977). (b) "Organizational and Personal Correlates of Attitudes toward Women as Managers". *Academy of Management Journal, 20,* no 1.

Thorsrud, E and Emery, F (1969). *Mot en nv bedriftsoraaniserina.* Oslo, Tanum.

Yin, R K (1984). *Case study research. Design and Methods.* Newbury Park, Sage.

Yukl, G (1981). *Leadership in organizations,* Engelwood-Cliffs, Prentice-Hall.

5

Teamworking: A Discussion of Issues from the Practitioner's Viewpoint: Workshop Discussions

Andrew Gale, Anthony Reid and Sue Cartwright

Introduction

This chapter reports on the workshops run at the conference upon which this book is based. The workshops were run following two of the three papers given at the conference. These are reproduced in Chapter 2 and Chapter 3. The committee members of the Women In Project Management Specific Interest Group (SIG) designed the workshop session with Anthony Reid of Management Achievement who acted as the facilitator for the workshop sessions at the conference. The SIG committee members all assisted in the facilitation of the six workshop groups. These groups constituted between six and seven delegates each, randomly selected by the conference organizers using a colour coding system. Hence the workshop groups and their themes are referred to in this chapter by colour (green, mauve, blue, yellow, red and brown).

The objectives of the workshops and their themes are explained. Key statements from the two speakers who gave papers immediately before the workshops session are presented. The six themes issued to the groups are listed and explained. Summaries of the reports back from the groups are given and a short discussion on issues arising from the workshop session is developed.

Objectives

The workshop session was designed to provide a period of time for delegates at the conference to explore some of the ideas being presented by speakers at the conference in a semi-structured way and to enable them to unravel some of the complex and intricate issues associated with effective team-working in the context of gender and organizational influences.

Delegates were also being given time to get to know a few of their fellow delegates and to make friends and connections. Delegates were given a brief which explained that groups should share their thoughts about the papers given by Thompson (Chapter 2) and Davidson (Chapter 3) and to integrate this with delegates' own experiences and ideas. The participating delegates represented a wide range of traditional and non-traditional project-based industries.

Groups were asked, as a particular challenge, to design a novel way of communicating their findings, output or results from their discussions, perhaps through mime, drama or illustration. The choice was left to the six individual groups.

A very important objective was for the groups to report back on the views, feelings and ideas of the whole group. This was not to be a majority position or a consensus but an inclusive statement reflecting minority positions and yet not appearing judgemental. The brief gave some pointers as to how this might be achieved. The SIG committee members who had worked together prior to the conference in preparation for the workshop session acted as facilitators and external raporteurs to each of the groups. They also observed the teamworking dynamics of each group but did not intervene or become heavily involved in the discussions of the groups. This part they all found very difficult but quite rewarding in that it provided self-awareness through lack of intervention and "allowed" them to listen to what was being said rather than planning how to intervene.

Key Points Made by Speakers Immediately Before the Workshop Session

PETER THOMPSON

Key points made by Peter Thompson included an emphasis that quality, in the context of management of complex and risk projects, was essentially that of the quality of the people involved in the teamworking and project management process, not the systems employed.

He stressed the need for rapid response and the ability to adapt to changing markets. This required precise communications. There was also now a growing need for a heightened and sharpened awareness of potential risks.

He argued for the need to provide opportunities for the development of both the individual and the team to which that individual belonged. This he linked with partnership arrangements where goals were jointly owned. He emphasized the importance of team leadership. This, he said, was not the sole responsibility of the project manager but should be shared by all members of the team directing the project.

Peter Thompson founded many of his arguments in the experience of the construction and engineering construction industry but constantly referred to the need for lateral thinking and the transfer of ideas and approaches across industries. "We should all be looking and learning from other industries", he said. With respect to the construction industry he argued that there is an opportunity for it to become more ordered, efficient and forward looking in the future – for it to transform.

MARILYN DAVIDSON

The main points made by Marilyn Davidson were that "self help" strategies for women are in reality only "sticking plaster" solutions. She argued that things were not actually getting better and that approaches aimed at helping women to "fit in" to a male world or work context were counterproductive and gained nothing for women or the organizations in which they work. Gender relationship and the impact of gender on group dynamics have implications for teamworking.

She said that increasing the number of women in the workplace does have a positive effect for the enhancement of women at work. However, this does not mean that attitudes do not need to be changed. She said that the work system needed to be changed to become gender inclusive.

Her overall position was that of a debunker of the many common myths which supported male dominance and control in society and the workplace.

Workshop Themes
The themes were characterized by statements given to each team (colour coded). Some of the statements presented to the teams were quite provocative.

Team Green
   "Mutual understanding between men and women leads to inferior team results".
Team Mauve
   "In what ways can the Women in Project Management SIG contribute towards an initiative of 'think manager, think qualified person?' "
Team Blue
   "The balanced team in a 20th century organization is made up of men plus women plus??"
Team Yellow
   "Women communicate – men shout. Who cares – get the job done!"
Team Red
   "Some of the key words relating to organizations at the

moment are performance, innovation, response and quality. In what way can project teams be best designed to meet these requirements and do women have a particular role to play?"

Team Brown

"Men will always dominate as leaders; women will always remain as followers. It's the law of nature."

This exercise could be usefully adapted and incorporated into team-building initiatives in a wider context.

Reports Back From the Workshop Teams

TEAM GREEN

"Mutual understanding between men and women leads to inferior team results". This team did not appoint or elect a leader or chair and proceeded in a fairly relaxed way, using the lunch break as a natural opportunity for creative thought and the development of good team relations. They did not stick rigidly to the brief, which they questioned, preferring to learn something about teamworking by following their own line of discussion and inquiry. The team appeared to work in three serial phases: agreeing their idea for action, allocating work equitably and getting their agreed tasks done.

The team was observed to maintain good interpersonal relations at the same time as challenging each other's opinions, views and approaches. They were arguably using conflict creatively without aggression, interpersonal conflict and negative emotion.

One issue the team identified was that projects could be relatively easily managed in a highly structured way through analysing the specification in reductionist way; by designing tasks and activities and managing resources against a pre-scribed time frame. However, they considered that it was more problematic to allow and in some way manage creative contributions and innovations to the project which might result in a change of direction part way through the project.

Team Presentation

The team made their presentation using posters in which they all had a role. Each poster indicated the chronology of the "phases" by using a clock face. These phases or stages were described as:

Birth
Immaturity
Adolescence
Maturity
Results

The Birth poster depicts thoughts and feelings characterised cryptically:

"Why are we here?"
"I'm confused!"
"I don't know what to think!"
"HELP!"
"GOSH!"
"What roles are people going to take?"

A person was shown having "facilitating thoughts". These statements speak for themselves, offering a strong feeling of "anxiety" and "open-endedness", of lack of direction. The team had a stressful birth experience.

The next poster, showing the Immaturity phase showed team members seated in a working circle with a flip chart at its centre. A facilitator was drawn. This could have been the observer. If so, she was considered a facilitator and that was a role she was supposed to adopt when necessary. Was she seen as a leader, in contradiction with the observer's own comment that no leader or chair was selected? This could mean that the team felt they had a facilitator and needed no leader. Did the team have a leader but was this person not easily identifiable by an outsider? This raises an interesting subtle question as to the nature, observability and definition of leadership and leaders in temporary teams. Someone was shown dozing and another asking the question: "What makes a good leader?" One participant was depicted as being energetic and one was shown leading the way to lunch. The interpretation one might draw from all this is that this phase was all about getting going and then taking a break to define the end of the beginning. This phase is characterized by questions and activity.

Lunch time was illustrated as the Adolescent phase. Nine smiling faces (including the observer/facilitator although not labelled such) were drawn seated around the circular lunch table. The single male member was identified wearing trousers. The statement appears: "It's not a gender issue", and all the team are shown to be having "bright" ideas. Obviously a happy and productive experience. Were they happy because it was lunch time or because of the ideas or both? The single statement indicates that the "issue" of gender was discussed but the question of what makes a good project team was perhaps not considered, by some anyway, to be related to gender or gendering. The sharing of social as well as essentially task-related activities has implications for effective team-working and the need to take occasional "time out".

The Maturity phase showed a happy team working hard in discussion writing things on their flip chart.

The final poster, with the phase entitled: Team Producing Quality (?!) Results, illustrated the team members all using their talents to produce their posters. The comments indicate that they were humorously proud of their creations and playing to their strengths.

> "If this was in the Tate Gallery people would pay thousands for it!"
> "Solved it!"
> "I'm good at printing."
> "I'll draw a beard then they'll know it's a man."

TEAM MAUVE

"In what ways can the Women in Project Management SIG contribute towards an initiative of 'think manager, think qualified person?' "

Five of the team members gave presentations as a form of feedback. This was carried out under the following headings:

Introduction
Barriers
Helpers
How to move forward

In introducing their presentations the team acknowledged that, at the current time, project management is associated with men but they all agreed that they were seeking to achieve "think manager, think qualified person". Interestingly, no men from the team were involved in presenting the team's findings.

Barriers
The working environment was identified as a significant, traditionally male factor. This was symbolized by the lack of amenities for women on most construction sites and normally the total lack of awareness and provision for women prior to and following pregnancy in the project management context. No clear definition of a manager was apparent and this contributed to the association with men and management. Further, it was seen as difficult to define the skills base of a project manager. It was argued that little regard was given to home life and family commitments by project managers and those in project teams. Men were said to resent women in a managerial position. It was suggested that men would not make way to or accommodate women without resistance. "Would turkeys vote for Christmas?"

Women appeared to lack the qualifications necessary for advancement in project management. This would tend to be corroborated by the support for a continuing professional development course entitled "Women in Project Management" funded by the European Union COMETT strand through WITEC. This was devised and organized by UMIST and The Association of Project Managers during 1994 in London. It was said that women had a low level of "self-belief" compared to men and even if women were relatively confident there were very few role models for them to observe as project managers.

The idea that there needed to be a "critical mass" of women in project management in order for a self-perpetuating process of increasing proportions of women in the discipline was discussed. It emerged that the team believed there to be an unfavourable pay differential between men and women in similar positions generally and that this is also reflected in project management.

Helpers

This team used the word "helpers" to describe factors that they considered to be of assistance in improving the position of women in project management. They asked the question: "What helpers do we have already?"

They felt that the recognition that there is a problem is a good start and the fact that the Association of Project Managers (APM) has a Specific Interest Group (SIG) "Women in Project Management" is also helpful.

They thought that because of the take up of high technology by project managers there was more emphasis on skills than strength; this was helpful to women. The team considered the increased application of information technology (IT) to be a notable "leveller".

An increase in the perceived number of role models in business at senior levels was seen as advantageous. There was, in their view, a growing acceptance of working women and developing legislation to support this situation.

The team argued that the publication of research which dispelled myths and challenged male attitudes towards women's traditional roles in society was beneficial.

How to Move forward

The team felt that it was important to involve men in the process of change necessary to improve women's position at work and in society.

The identification of the *actual* attributes and associated sets of skills necessary for a given job function required to perform in that job was seen as an important way of supporting equality of opportunity.

The publication of job opportunities should be done in an open and accessible way in order to ensure that women and men are aware of new positions.

There should be a positive and active approach towards the promotion of the role of women in project management through initiatives such as work in schools, careers presentations, workshops, mentoring and training courses.

TEAM BLUE

"The balanced team in a 20th century organization is made up of men plus women plus??"

The notes from the observer/facilitator for this group allow a real insight into the development of discussion that occurred in this team. There is a brief report on the development of the team's discussions, followed by their report back.

The team discussed whether the theme should not be concerned with people rather than men plus women. One view was that to talk of men and women in this context was confrontational. They also discussed the question of discrimination, asking: "Why is it so important?"

The issue of "getting the balance right" featured several times during the discussions. What constitutes a balance of characteristics, in this context what makes a good leader, and does a balanced team mean a successful team? One view was that women had to fight and it is now time to concentrate on balance.

One person said that women look at things differently (from men). There was some debate about whether or not women "actually do think of women as acting differently". A view was put that "women should feel free to act in different ways and wear dresses". Women were seen by some to be more adaptable (than men), learning to be flexible early in their lives. An argument was made that women can use femininity and masculinity to their advantage in particular situations.

Discussion focused on the nature of a particular job and who was qualified to do that job. Age and qualifications were considered relevant. It was argued that the right team will vary depending on the project environment.

There were mixed views as to whether gender was important or not. Pregnancy was discussed and a view was put that women and the organization can prepare for this. Some participants asked what men do to prepare for the pregnancy of their partner with respect to commitment at work. A view was expressed that "women's role" should not obstruct project objectives.

It emerged that one project organization circulated details of the conference to women in the organization only. Some of the team were shocked by this. There was a view expressed that having a Women in Project Management Specific Interest Group (SIG) in the APM was wrong because it put people off and discriminated against men. The statement was made by one team member that "women managers are not feminists".

Team Presentation
The team were all women. They all agreed that they tended to share similar views. Their underpinning points of view were that there was no difference between men and women. The right team is the balanced team with the right people. They presented their findings under a number of headings.

Task of a Team
It was argued that there is only a biological/physical difference between men and women. There are examples of tasks where a man undertakes traditionally female work and this is not liked by women (e.g. midwifery). Therefore, perhaps in the context of other professions and occupations, the work culture may inhibit male participation.

Culture/Environment
Organizational culture and environment were considered to be

important factors in team formation. The culture (nationally, industrially and organizationally) influenced how women were regarded.

Personalities

The team cannot consist exclusively of leaders. Personality was considered an important variable. Some people just quietly work hard. All teams need leaders and followers. Some people are not good at expressing but are excellent at implementing the ideas of others. Individuals play different roles in different teams.

Resources

The best person for the job should not be determined by the sex of applicants. The "old boy network" still dominates in the project management environment. Ageist and stereotypical attitudes are common. Men are "frightened" of being taken out to lunch by women in case their wives find out. An example of sex stereotyping was that when using the name "Steve" a woman was able to get more calls returned than when she used "Stephanie". The point was made that teams have to make the best with what they have.

Mix of Skills and Qualities

The question could be asked: "What do men bring to team environments?" Men tend to accept the leadership role and women deal with conflict. Women calm things down and inject humour into a difficult situation. Women can lighten things and have the ability to laugh at themselves and display a sense of enjoyment and enthusiasm. For things to be different would mean men losing face. Men are "allowed" to be "bolshy" due to socially-determined norms of behaviour. Teams vary according to the relative proportions of men and women. For a team to work effectively it has to "gel". Social issues and work can be separated but "social" constraints can prevent or affect promotion when people are in conflict. Conflict is good if it is controlled and managed.

Conclusions

A team can be in any combination of men and women to be good. A bad team can be improved by adding another member with special qualities. Gender is not the answer.

TEAM YELLOW

"Women communicate – men shout. Who cares – get the job done!"

The team discussed the meaning of "shout" and interpreted it as "heavy handed approach". Men were seen to manipulate and be less polite than women. It was argued that women want to maintain and repair relationships whereas men are less inclined to be this way.

Team Presentation

Women were said to communicate better than men. This was associated with a difference in management style between men and women. The typical management approaches of men and women were compared, using "snagging" as an example. Snagging is the process of listing items needing rectification in building work at the end of a project. Men, it was said, find fault with things in order to have them put right. Women were argued to assume the trades-people had done their best and were therefore more constructive in their criticism.

In an apparently contradictory statement the team said that the approach to the issue of effective teams was not related to gender; project management being all about leadership and communication.

TEAM RED

"Some of the key words relating to organizations at the moment are performance, innovation, response and quality. In what way can project teams be best designed to meet these requirements and do women have a particular role to play?"

The feedback from this team was based on a great deal of

discussion. They decided to analyse the words carefully and spent a lot of time on defining sex and gender. They felt that for them "innovation had a day off!"

Quality was discussed as a pertinent issue. It was said that one person's quality was not the same as another person's quality.

The general view was that project team selection was a key issue and this should be based on the principle of the best person for the job. Task, team and individual variables were overlapping and demonstrated by Fig. 1.

TEAM BROWN

"Men will always dominate as leaders; women will always remain as followers. It's the law of nature".

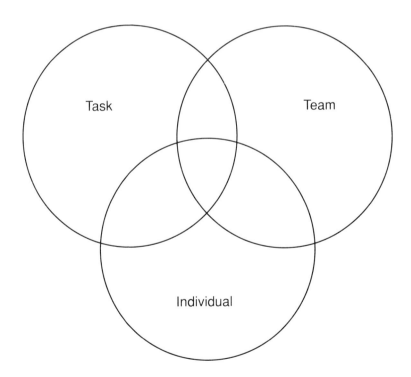

Fig. 1 Project team: Task, Team and Individual variables

The facilitator for this team said that they started as all female and were joined by a man.

The team thought it had a sense of balance – women and men working together. The team appeared balanced in relation to skill needs.

The team discussed the changing emphasis from physical to intellectual needs of effective teams. They identified the importance of process being necessary within a team prior to being able to work together, allowing creativity and interpersonal skills to flourish.

Team Presentation

One of the team gave an overhead presentation of the team's findings. The first statement made was that "we should forget dominance of women by men". This set the tone for the rest of the team's presentation.

The team decided the focus should be on leadership and that leadership was not management. They came up with ten characteristics, which they said people perceived as naturally associated with leaders by sex.

		MEN	WOMEN
1	Ambition	*	
2	Perception		*
3	Communication		*
4	Experience	*	
5	Flexibility		*
6	Admit mistakes		*
7	Empathy		*
8	Morality		*
9	Tenacity	*	
10	Survival	*	*

Closing Discussion

The convenor of the workshop session directed discussion in the following areas:

Consideration of the whole team
Direct influences
Indirect influences
Expectations
Sources of power and influence

Belbin's model (1981) was put forward as a useful device for identifying dominant role and possible team structures. This model is based on an American study of teamworking and is concerned with compatibility and the need for leadership in a single person. Belbin lists eight roles necessary for a team to be effective. The Myers-Briggs Type Indicator was cited as a method for assessing the suitability or otherwise of a team member.

Summary of Issues

Briefly identified below are the main issues arising from the teams' processes and output. They all showed remarkable similarity in many ways.

The teams in this workshop session were all, to a greater or lesser extent, observed to go through various phases from inception through completion of their short lives. The team process was considered by the conference organizers to be important as well as the "findings" from each team. These phases have been identified by others and are the subject of research. Langford *et al* (1995) refer to this with respect to contingency theories of leadership, arguing that effective project team performance depends upon situational factors.

The importance of leaders and leadership emerged as a strong theme in virtually all groups, both with respect of the teams themselves and the subject of their discussions. Organizational culture in the context of national and industry cultures and project environmental factors were also mentioned frequently. Schein (1985) argues that leadership and culture are "opposite sides of the same coin". Although communication was mentioned by many as fundamental to effective teamworking, it is argued by Handy (1993) that communication is a symptom of organizational health and not a primary cause of effectiveness.

The balance of teams in terms of sex, skills and the qualities of team members was a strong theme taken up during the discussion stage following the team feedbacks by the workshop convenor. Belbin (1981) argues that all the team functions his research identifies must be present in an effective team. Most teams stressed the importance of appropriate selection criteria based on task analysis of project functions.

It was said by some and implied by others that a "critical mass" of women would bring about change in organizational culture, working practices and the likely increase in the proportion of women in project management. The argument for role models and initiatives to encourage more women to enter project management disciplines was made by several people. There is by no means consensus among researchers on this subject. There is no concrete evidence to support the critical mass argument. Initiatives, aimed at increasing the proportion of women in traditionally male occupations, such as "Insight Programmes" are effective but some have suggested that they may act as a sort of filter, supporting sterotypical career selection such as school students self-selecting on the basis of what they feel they will fit into rather than finding equality of opportunity through the information and insights provided (Gale 1994).

Insight courses were conceived by the British Engineering Industry Training Board (EITB) in 1979 as one week long residential summer schools attracting high achieving female school students. Key features of these courses were industrial visits and female role model group leaders. More details on the structure and evaluation of these courses are noted in Peacock and Eaton (1987), Peacock and Shinkins (1983) and Viscardi (1987).

Several teams made the argument that effective team-working was nothing to do with gender. This was contradicted in many ways by earlier and later references to differences between men and women and their management style and approaches to leadership and communication. Further, participants obviously experienced difficulty in getting to grips with the argument that organizations can be understood as gendered. The concept that organizations viewed through a "gender lens" may allow new explanations of behaviour uncovers new variables, enhancing analytic opportunities. A contributing factor may be that women in male-dominated occupations, such as construction management, frequently assert that they are not feminists and do not agree with feminism. This is supported by research findings (Gale 1994). Many of the predominantly female conference participants are likely to have rejected notions of feminism as they were largely drawn from male-dominated industries such as construction, transport and engineering, although finance and consultancy, non-traditional project management industries, were also represented.

The involvement of men in strategies and action for the future inclusion of women in project management was seen by most participants as a good thing. It could be argued that what is good for men is good for women (Gale 1991).

References

Belbin, A M (1981). *Management Teams*. Heinemann.

Gale, A W (1991). "What is good for women is good for men: theoretical foundations for action research aimed at increasing the proportion of women in construction management." In Barret, P and Males, R (eds) *Practice Management: New Perspectives for the Construction Professional*. Chapman and Hall, London, 26–34.

Gale, A W (1994). "Women in Construction: An investigation into some aspects of image and knowledge as determinants of the under representation of women in construction management in the British construction industry", PhD Thesis, University of Bath.

Handy C (1993). *Understanding Organizations*. Penguin, Harmondsworth.

Langford D, Hancock, M Fellows, R and Gale, A W (1995). *Human Resources Management in Construction*. Longmans, London.

Peacock, S and Shinkins, S (1983). *Insight: A review of the Insight Programme to encourage more girls to become professional engineers*. OP10 EITB, Watford.

Peacock, S and Eaton, C (1987). *Women in Engineering EITB Initiatives*. *RC19*, EITB, Watford.

Schein, E H (1985). *Organizational Culture and Leadership*. San Francisco: Jossey Bass.

Viscardi, K (1987). *Insight: Encouraging girls to become professional engineers. EITB RC18*. EITB, Watford.

6

Conclusions and Research Agenda

Andrew Gale and Sue Cartwright

Introduction
This chapter reviews the key issues arising in the body of this book. The future of the project team is briefly discussed, arguing the need for a two team system as put forward by Thompson, who also stresses the importance of the quality of people in the project team. The under-representation of women in project management is identified, citing construction as a traditional project management industry displaying masculine characteristics, with a conflictual and crisis-ridden environment. The gendering of organizations is an important concept giving an insight into the functioning and dysfunctioning of organizations of value to the project manager. Myths about women managers and women at work are reviewed and debunked. The reaction of project management practitioners, as participants of the day conference where the papers forming this book were given, are discussed. An agenda for research into women in project management and the gendering of project management is tentatively suggested. Finally an argument is made for "gender inclusive" project management in the future.

Project Teams of the Future

Projects are becoming more complex, with increasingly diverse players, stake holders and influences, both internal and external. This causes fragmentation in the management of projects. The client's role is becoming more complex and difficult to define. Project scope definition and the needs of the client may change during the life of a project, creating the need for more attention to be paid to the management of the subsequent risks generated for the project and necessity for flexibility to be built into the project management process.

Investment in the project team is an important consideration in reducing and managing risks and uncertainty to ensure clients' needs are met. The client's role is changing and this means that the boundary between the management of the project and the management of the client organization is becoming necessarily blurred. This brings with it ambiguity and contradiction as the needs and objectives of the sponsoring organization and the project organization cannot and should not be identical. The project has a temporary organization; the sponsoring organization is permanent in orientation. Further, through undertaking a project the sponsor may well become involved in matters of political or environmental sensitivity. These need to be managed and responded to in an intelligent and appropriate way. These matters cannot be systematized; they generally require appropriate human inter-actions and complex "fuzzy" solutions.

The public importance of a project can mean that there is a need for significant input from a public relations function dealing with political and image factors. The client needs to invest in the project management function to achieve a number of objectives: risk reduction, appropriate functional outcomes, value for money and conflict-free relations with partners and other players.

This all means that the client is an important "driving" player in the management of projects, needing to ensure that the direction, priorities, objectives and scope are clearly represented in a timely way to those implementing the project. This gives rise to the need for two teams: one which Thompson defines as the Project Board, responsible for appraisal and the overseeing of implementation and commissioning. The second is the more traditional concept of the Project Management Team, responsible for the implementation of the project. Thompson argues for the increased use of partnering and alliance contracts in the future, designed to promote and enhance teamworking between clients and contractors. Teamworking and a project manager's personal attributes of positive attitude, good judgement and decision making, adaptability and behavioural understanding are key factors for successful project management.

Homogeneous v Heterogeneous Project Teams
In order for a team to be effective, it needs to clearly define its overall goals and objectives from the outset. It has been suggested that this role should be undertaken by a project board which is separate and different from the traditional project management team.

In the course of implementation, the Project Management Team will need to establish new systems and procedures, break down the task into more specific and discrete goals and accommodate the input of a diverse range of stakeholder interests. At the same time it has to be mindful of the time and budgetary constraints under which it has to operate. This can present a major dilemma to member selection and team functioning. Homogeneous groups are recognized to be most effective at performing tasks which are relatively simple, where speed is important and high levels of co-operation are demanded. On the other hand, heterogeneous groups are more suited to complex tasks, where speed is not an issue and a high level of creativity is required. Projects are typically characterised by complexity, time pressures, and a need for both creativity and co-operation; hence their considerable potential for conflict both internal (within the team) and external (between the team and the client organization).

For the team to be effective it needs to reach a level of group maturity, whereby it fully utilizes its combined resources, recognizes and accepts the strengths and weaknesses of its individual members and energizes the commitment and motivation of the whole team. Within the project management environment, diversity and co-operation have to be nurtured. Because the discipline and techniques of project management originated in traditional industries like construction and engineering, there has been as carryover of the culture and norms characteristically associated with these industries into the project environment.

A major theme which has emerged from this conference is that project management teams tend towards a homogeneous culture which is demonstrably masculine in orientation. It has been argued that this can operate to exclude and stifle the contribution of certain individuals, particularly women.

The Under-Representation of Women in Project Management
There are no statistical data concerning the sex distribution of project managers and project management functions. Some data are available for the construction industry but these do not identify project management. However, as the data below illustrate, women are under-represented in a traditional project management environment.

In terms of the horizontal sex segregation of the labour market, women represented 6.7 per cent (EOC 1988) of the full-time workforce in 1981. No reliable vertical segregation data are gathered currently. The Construction Industry

Table 1: Vertical occupational segregation of the construction industry sector by sex (percentages)

Occupation	Male	Female	1971 Total	Male	Female	1981 Total
Managers	6.9	5.1	6.8	8.7	8.4	8.7
Technicians	4.2	0.6	4.0	5.0	1.3	4.8
Secretarial & sim	3.2	88.6	8.2	2.8	82.2	9.1
Supervisory	4.8	1.6	4.6	4.9	1.7	4.6
Crafts	51.7	1.1	48.8	54.2	3.0	50.1
Operatives	15.6	2.3	14.8	15.0	2.5	14.0
Others	13.6	0.7	12.8	9.4	0.9	8.7
Totals employed	94.2	5.8	100.0	92.0	8.0	100.0

Sources: General census data 1971 and 1981 (Rainbird 1989) analyzed by Gale (Gale, 1991)

Training Board (CITB) does not gather data on the construction industry workforce by sex. However, an analysis of 1981 General Census data shows that only 8.4 per cent (Rainbird 1989) of women in the construction industry occupy managerial positions. Just over 82 per cent of them were employed in secretarial or clerical jobs.

The low proportion of women in built environment and other male-dominated sectors is reflected in higher education (Beacock and Pearson 1989). The percentage of female building undergraduates at British universities (not including old polytechnics) rose from 9 per cent in 1985/86 to 13 per cent in 1990/91. Polytechnic (now new universities) entrants to building degrees showed a small rise from 7 per cent in 1985/86 to 8 per cent in 1990/91, with a high of 10 per cent in 1988/89.

Table 3 demonstrates the male characteristics of construction industry professions, with only 40 female corporate members of the Chartered Institute of Building (CIOB) out of 8,452 in 1992 and 594 women out of a total of 32,562 in all grades (CIOB 1992). The CIOB is attempting to address this situation, a point demonstrated by the fact that these data are a function of the Institute's self-critical review. A Women in Building Consultative Committee meets annually to discuss this question. Women account for less than 4 per cent of the institution of Civil Engineers (ICE) and 3.2 per cent of the Royal Institution of Chartered Surveyors (RICS) (Quantity Division) (Greed 1991).

Gender and Gendering
Gender and the gendering of cultures has been little considered by organizational theorists until quite recently. The terms sex and gender are often confused. Sex is a biological type. Individuals are born having a male or female sex type. However, gender is socially constructed (Garett 1987) and subsequently learnt. Because it is socially constructed, individuals (men and women) may tend to be more male or female in a gender sense. There is, of course, a strong association between biological sex type and gender values. Once uncoupled from biological sex, as has been discussed, the concept

Table 2: Membership of some construction industry professional bodies in 1992

Professional Bodies	All Grades M	F	Corporate M	F	Fellows M	F
Chartered Institute of Building	31,968 (98.2)	594 (1.8)	8,412 (99.5)	40 (0.5)	2,280 (99.9)	2 (0.1)
Royal Institution Chartered Survey's*	83,555 (92.7)	6,575 (7.3)	37,638 (92.5)	3,043 (7.5)	26,141 (99.4)	159 (0.6)
Institution of Civil Engineers	76,423 (96.8)	2,497 (3.2)	43, 027 (99.0)	416 (1.0)	6,174 (99.9)	5 (0.1)

Sources: The membership departments of each institution. (CIOB 1992) (percentages in parentheses).

of gender can be applied to cultures as having a masculine/ feminine dimension. It is suggested that masculine cultures are likely to be dominated by power-relationships and are results oriented. Feminine cultures are likely to be more concerned with interpersonal relationships and be process oriented. Power cultures are likely to be experienced by the majority of men and women as being less satisfying than task or team cultures which place a greater emphasis on expert knowledge rather than positional power and allow members more individual autonomy.

Different culture types promote and nurture different managerial styles. Power cultures, which it is suggested epitomize masculinity, are characterized by command structures and expect employees to "do what they are told without questioning". They are also highly politicized environments and operate on the axiom of "survival of the fittest". There has been substantial research comparing the managerial style of men and women (Alimo-Metcalfe 1993). Overall, a few differences have been identified. A recent unpublished study (Ferrario 1990) of 124 female managers and 95 male managers found that women had a significantly more team management style than men, characterized by a high regard for people and a high regard for task. Vinnicombe (1987) found that compared with males, women are less "traditional" and more "visionary" in their approach to business; a valuable asset to any organization. It is suggested that the problems encountered and discomfort experienced by women working in masculine power cultures may not necessarily be different from that of many male colleagues in terms of job attributes. However, traditionally men may find it easier to accept or at least overtly comply with the structure, constraints and values which characterize such cultures. Evidence suggests that women respond in the same way as men to unmet expectations, but have particular difficulty and lack preparedness in dealing with highly politicized organizational environments (Rosin and Karabik 1991; Harragan 1977). Compared with men, women may have a heightened sense of awareness and a greater sense of cultural incongruence and gender exclusion.

Myths about Women at Work and in Management Debunked
Davidson lists a number of commonly held myths concerning women and work and management. She cites a number of research-based arguments to debunk these myths. These include the notion that pregnancy is the main reason for women managers leaving organizations.

There are very few differences by sex regarding achievement, motivation and promotion and some findings show that in certain cases women can be more ambitious than men.

Some studies show women to be more committed than men in the work organization. Women are not less mobile than men in the labour market and often make more radical job-related changes and are more adaptable.

In terms of leadership women are not shown as inferior to men. Indeed there are more similiarities than dissimiliarities between male and female leaders. Compare this with the differences reported by Team Brown (Chapter 5). It might be more accurate to define certain characteristics as female and male in a gender sense (arising in men and/or women).

Leadership, according to Schein (1985), cannot be discussed without reference to organizational culture. Culture and leadership are opposite sides of the same coin. A key component of organizational culture is gender. Kvande and Davidson both address the importance of the gendering of organizations. Leadership is a key component of project management so it follows that the gendering of project management is an important consideration for students of project management and project managers.

The male values underpinning common practice in project management today include long working hours, separation between work and family commitments (often expressed as total commitment) and sex role stereotyping with respect to occupational segregation in project teams.

The "smart macho" culture is one in which managers feel under such pressure to reach performance targets that they encourage excessively long working hours in their organizations. This is a common feature of construction culture.

Gale (1994b) argues that in construction, characterized by masculinity, crisis and conflict, it will be difficult to change the culture because people "joined" the industry to be a part of this culture or learned to "fit in".

Davidson argues that too often it can be demonstrated that we "think manager, think (white) male". The workshop response to this was that we should think manager, think qualified person. The qualifications should relate to the requirements for good project management of teams, as discussed above, based on the factors put forward by Thompson, stressing the importance of human relationships and interactions, reduction in conflict, increased collaboration, good teamworking and people-orientated solutions.

Organizational Culture and Gender
Various typologies have been suggested as a means of usefully describing differences in culture between organizations. Harrison (1972; 1986) suggests four main types of organizational culture: power, role, task/achievement and person/support. Deal and Kennedy (1982) have also proposed four

generic culture types as being determined exclusively by one aspect of organizational behaviour, that is the degree and the speed of feedback on whether decisions or strategies are successful. Hofstede (1980) analysed culture differences between nationalities and suggested that culture had four dimensions: power distance, uncertainty avoidance, individualism/collectivism and masculinity/femininity. According to Mant (1983) Anglo-Saxon bloc countries such as USA, UK and Australia tend towards masculinity and individualism. In contrast, Scandinavian bloc countries such as Sweden, Denmark and Norway tend towards more feminine cultures whilst still retaining a high degree of individualism. More recently Hofstede *et al* (1990) conducted a study of the culture of the 20 organizations in Denmark and the Netherlands and concluded that differences between organizations in terms of their practices, that is conventions, customs, habits and mores, can be considered on the following dimensions:

(i)   process orientated *v* results oriented
(ii) employee orientated *v* job orientated
(iii) parochial *v* professional – dependent upon whether employees derive their identity from the organizatiaon (parochial) or from the type of job they perform (professional)
(iv) open *v* closed systems of communication
(v)   loose *v* tight control – dependent on the degree of formal internal structure
(vi) normative *v* pragmatic – dependent upon whether customer orientation is market driven (pragmatic) or the organization perceives its attitude towards the outside world as the implementation of inviolable rules (normative).

With the exception of (ii) and (iv), which are considered to be related to the philosophy of culture founders and leaders, an organization's relative position on these dimensions is considered to be the outcome of the type of business activity in which it is engaged. Using the typology originally proposed by Harrison, studies have investigated the impact of culture and culture change on the organizational commitment, job satisfaction and psychological wellbeing of organizational members working in various industries (Cartwright and Cooper 1989; Cartwright and Cooper 1992). Such research indicates that individuals working in organizational cultures which are incongruent with their individual cultural preference or values express a greater propensity to leave and are more likely to experience low job satisfaction and psychological ill health. Furthermore, organizational cultures which place a high degree of constraint on the individual and offer little autonomy are generally experienced by the majority of employees, irrespective of sex, as less satisfying and potentially more stressful. Perceptions of control and loss of autonomy are frequently cited as major reasons for voluntary decisions to leave organizations following changes in ownership or culture (Hayes and Hoag 1974).

Based on a study of male and female engineers in six industries in Norway, Kvande and Rasmussen (1992) differentiate between two types of organization: static hierarchies and dynamic networks. Static hierarchies are described as an old fashioned system in which older males maintain patriarchial power relations. In contrast, dynamic network organizations are ones in which the dominant male group are young men who form alliances with "new" women, who are similar to themselves in work orientation and motivation. These young alliances usurp the old men. According to Kvande and Rasmussen, women get on better in these organizations compared with static hierarchies because:

> In dynamic networks the work is organized in teams where all contribute knowledge and effort on an equal basis. As they work, the graduate engineers get to know each other's academic and personal qualifications. The women become visible as professionals for their colleagues and superiors.

Roger Pauli (1989), Group Managing Director of Stuart Crystal, addressing the Women's Education Conference, suggested that as, historically, organizational structures have been devised within a male-dominated society, they have been based on a military model and are primarily command structures. According to Pauli, in a command structure: "thinking was done at the top and people lower down in the organization were not expected to think about what they did'. Gale (1994a) suggests that it is meaningful to describe certain professions and industry cultures such as construction, which is demonstrably male in terms of horizontal sex segregation, as being "macho" or masculine cultures. All of these terms, static hierarchies, command structures and macho cultures can be summatively characterized as power cultures (Harrison 1972) which place the highest degree of constraint on individuals comparative to other culture types.

The Reaction of Practitioners
The workshop team participants (Chapter 5) were mainly project management practitioners of one sort or another from "traditional" and "non-traditional" industries. Findings from the teams were in many cases contradictory in that gender was not seen as relevant but there were a number of indications where it was relevant. Further, the struggle for equal opportunities at work and the legislation supporting this position have all come about through the vociferous arguments of women about women's rights over a long period of time (Meehan 1985; Spender 1983).

Feedback relating to interventions from Davidson and Kvande, who both certainly argued the importance and relevance of gender and gendering in organizations and society, were well received by a majority of participants. Evidence from anecdotes told during the workshop sessions and throughout the conference indicate that women's experience in project management requires them to "fit in" to a greater or lesser extent. This is supported by Gale's findings (1994b).

One interpretation of the responses of the participants is that they generally did not see why sex should make a difference and would express this as "think manager, think qualified person". In other words they were arguing that organizations should be gender-blind. This would be relevant if the societal roles of men and women were similar. The dissimilarity between the societal roles and underpinning societal values with respect to men and women means that gender-blind approaches discriminate against women.

"Gender-blind" organizational cultures are not common in the private sector but some individual managers may take a gender-blind perspective. These are organizations in which men have learnt to speak the new language of equality. These organizations are highly politicized. Political correctness is the currency of power and the basis for judging others. This is the culture of the "feminist pretender" with "experts" on equality. This type can probably only be found in some public sector construction organizations (Maddock and Parkin 1993).

An Agenda for Research
As organizations continue to encounter complex, unprecedented and indivisible tasks and problems which a single individual or organization cannot accomplish or resolve alone, project management teams will increasingly become a feature of organizational life. Unfortunately, project management and the dynamics of teamworking is an under-researched area. It would therefore seem appropriate to close this chapter by setting out a research agenda of issues which may have an influence on the culture, practices and performance of project management teams.

A) TRADITIONAL V NON-TRADITIONAL PROJECT BASED INDUSTRIES
An argument can be made for classifying industries using project management techniques as either traditional or non-traditional. Industries which are traditionally associated with project management techniques may include: construction, heavy engineering, process and petrochemical, power, utilities, transport and defence. Non-traditional industries may be: finance, health, training, research and development, IT and consultancy. Traditional industries have arguably always been project based. Non-traditional industries may only use project management techniques and project teams.

B) PUBLIC AND PRIVATE SECTOR ORGANIZATIONS
Public sector industries and organizations may differ in practice and organization with respect to project management compared with private sector industries.

C) SOCIALISATION OF THE PROJECT ENVIRONMENT
If women and men are being socialised to "fit in" to organizational cultures through education and industrial influences the influence of work group dynamics and membership is likely to have a pervasive impact on the values and behaviour of female entrants to an industry. This issue is probably central to the topic of women in project management.

D) THE INFLUENCE OF GENDER ON WORK CULTURE
Women working in a project management function are not necessarily project managers. The clerical or secretarial function in a project team is traditionally undertaken by women. The gendering of work through semantic changes with respect to job titles should be carefully considered by research in this subject.

The different adjectives used to characterize and describe the identical behaviours and actions of men and women may give an important insight into the gendering of work.

There will almost certainly be cross-cultural differences in the relative importance of these items nationally and "local" variations in focus will be expected. Methodological approaches adopted might vary depending on the preferences and disciplines of researchers. A variety of approaches could be creative, provided there is general agreement about the frame of reference provided by common issues and questions being researched. Initially, at least, researchers may find it worthwhile to evaluate and refine these issues and questions in the context of a discourse on definitions, for example, the definition of project management and managers and the question of traditional and non-traditional industries.

Women into Project Management
Attracting more women into project management will also

attract more men because a "gender inclusive" project environment will be just that. It will not be exclusive. Many of the reasons why women feel excluded or feel that there are barriers are the same for men too. Research into women in project management needs to be undertaken to expand understanding of gender relations in the project environment. Gender is not just about women; it is about both sexes. By using a "gender lens" to view and interpret project organizations and project firms and industries new perspectives will emerge. This will lead to higher quality, better management of resources and will add to our understanding of cost and time relationships. It is through people that organizational objectives are achieved.

Organizational cultures vary but are all gendered. Even the gender-blind culture in which there may be a sincere commitment to remove barriers for women does not acknowledge the reality of women's working lives. Women's working lives do not develop in a vacuum. They are a function of the gendered relations in society, industry and work.

It is essential that the significance of gender and project management be studied, understood, discussed and used. This will help develop professionalism in project management and enhance the lessons that can be learnt from investigating project management in whichever industries it is practised. Insights and theory developed through focusing on women in project management can potentially add to the education and training of project managers.

References

Alimo-Metcalfe, B (1993). "Women in Business and Management – The United Kingdom" in M J Davidson and C L Cooper (Eds) *European Women in Business & Management*, Paul Chapman Publishing, London.

Beacock, P M and Pearson, J S D (1989). *Characteristics of Higher Education for the Construction Professions: Development Services Project Report 24*. CNAA, London 96–7.

CIOB (1992). *Appendix A Document AU(WIBCC)823*. CIOB, Ascot.

Cartwright, S and Cooper, C L (1989). "Predicting Success in Joint Venture Organizations in Information Technology – a cultural perspective". *Journal of General Management, 15*, 39–52.

Cartwright, S and Cooper, C L (1992). *Mergers & Acquisitions: The Human Factor.* Oxford: Butterworth & Heinemann.

Cartwright, S and Gale, A W (1995). "Project Management: Different gender, different culture? – A discussion paper on gender and organizational culture Part II" in *Leadership & Organizational Development Vol. 16 (4) 12–17 (in press).*

Deal and Kennedy (1982). *Corporate Culture: The Rites and Rituals of Corporate Life.* London: Penguin Business.

EOC (1988) Women and men in Britain a research profile. HMSO, London, 37.

Ferrario, M (1990). "Leadership Styles of British Men & Women Managers". Unpublished MSc Dissertation, University of Manchester Institute of Science & Technology, Manchester.

Gale, A W (1991). "What is good for women is good for men: Theoretical foundations for action research aimed at increasing the proportion of women in construction management" in Barrett, P and Males, R (eds) *Practice Management: New perspectives for the construction professional.* Chapman and Hall, London, 26–34.

Gale, A W (1992). "The construction industry's male culture must feminize if conflict is to be reduced: The role of education as a gatekeeper to a male construction industry." In Fenn, P and Gameson, R (eds) *Construction Conflict: Management and Resolution.* F N Spon, London, 416–27.

Gale, A W (1994a). "*Women in Non-traditional Occupations: The Construction Industry*", in Women in Management Review, Vol 9, No. 2, 3–14.

Gale, A W (1994b) "Women in Construction: An investigation into some aspects of image and knowledge as determinants of the under representation of women in

construction management in the British construction
industry", PhD Thesis – University of Bath.

Gale, A W and Cartwright, S (1995). "Women in Project
Management: Entry into a Male Domain" – A discussion
paper on gender and organizational culture Part I" in
Leadership & Organizational Development Vol. 16 (2) 4–
9.

Garret, S (1987). *Gender.* London, Tavistock Publications.

Greed, C (1991). *Surveying Sisters, Women in a traditional male
profession.* Routledge, London, 3–24, 51, 105–22.

Harragan, B L (1977). *Games Mother Never Taught You.* New
York, Warner.

Harrison, R (1972). "How to describe your organization".
Harvard Business Review. May/June. 5 1 119–128.

Harrison, R (1987). "Organizational culture and the quality
of service". *Association for Management Education &
Development.* London.

Hayes, R H and Hoag, G H (1974). "Post acquisition
retention of top management". *Mergers & Acquisitions*, 9,
8–18.

Hofstede, G (1980). *Culture's Consequences.* Sage.

Hofstede, G, Neuijen, B, Daval, O and Sanders, G (1990).
"Measuring organizational cultures; A qualitative and
quantitative study across twenty cases". *Administrative
Science Quarterly*, *35*, 286–316.

Kvande, E and Rasmussen, B (1992). "Structures – politics
–cultures; Understanding the gendering of organizations"
in Proceedings of GASAT East and West European
Conference. Eindhoven, October 25–29.

Langford, D A Fellows, R F, Hancock, M and Gale, A W
(1995). Human Resources Management In Construction,
Longman Higher Education, London

Maddock, S and Parkin, D (1993) "Gender cultures:
Women's choices and strategies at work". In Women in
Management Review. Bradford, MCB University Press
Ltd, Vol, 8 No. 2 3–9.

Mant, A (1993). *Leaders We Deserve*

Meehan, E M (1985). *Women's rights at work: campaign and*

policy in Britain and the United States. London, Macmillan, 70–1.

Pauli, R (1989). "Masculine Management in Industry in Harnessing the Female Resource". The Women's Education Conference of 1989, report of the Conference held at Queen Elizabeth II Conference Centre, July 11, London, *Women in Management.* 22–3.

Rainbird, H (1989) *Personal communications*

Roslin, H M and Karabik, K (1991). "Workplace variables, affective responses and intention to leave among women managers". *Journal of Occupational Psychology, 64(4),* 317–331.

Schein, E H (1985). *Organizational Culture and Leadership.* San Francisco, Jossey Bass.

Spender, D (1983). "Modern feminists theorists reinventing rebellion." In Spender, D. (ed) *Feminist Theorists.* The Women's Press, London, 366–80.

Vinnicombe, S (1987). "What exactly are the differences in male and female working styles?" *Women in Management Review, Vol 3, 1,* 13–21.

Index